The Muslim Mindset

Practical Lessons in Achieving a Positive Mental Attitude

I dedicate this book to my father, my sole inspiration and compass for navigating through life.

To my mother: If all the oceans were ink, it would still not be sufficient to describe what you mean to me.

To Edriss: For your ability to see the brightest stars in the foggiest hours.

To Raissa: Forever attached at the hip inshallah ☺

To Ruquia: The most insightful soul I have ever known.

To my genius little sister Mariam: For letting me bother you at all hours of the day and night, and somehow, still waiting to hear my next crazy idea with just as much enthusiasm.

To Asiya: My favorite little author and storyteller.

To Fatimah/Juwairiah Ansari: For your encouragement and strange ways of motivating me. Can't complain.

To every person who has been kind, encouraging and a positive force in my life. May Allah grant you the best of both worlds. Ameen.

CONTENTS

- 1 | **Introduction**
- 12 | **What is the Muslim Mindset?**
- 20 | LESSON 1:
  Increase Your Eman
- 43 | LESSON 2:
  Lower Your Wings of Humility for Your Parents
- 52 | LESSON 3:
  Keep Good Company
- 65 | LESSON 4:
  Practice Forgiveness Daily
- 80 | LESSON 5:
  Keep Your Health Intact
- 93 | LESSON 6:
  Think Positive
- 111 | LESSON 7:
  Wake Up Early
- 121 | LESSON 8:
  Practice Gratitude Daily
- 131 | LESSON 9:
  Strive Towards Patience
- 141 | LESSON 10:
  Execute Your Goals
- 175 | **Glossary**
- 178 | **Bibliography**

Introduction

BEFORE my family and I stepped off of the airplane, we knew that our lives would never be the same. We had arrived in what we considered to be the land of opportunity, "America the great, America the beautiful."

The idea of living in the West made some of us feel like anything is possible. This is precisely the *vibe* that America creates in many who live abroad, dreaming of one day being of the fortunate ones to feel its breeze on their faces.

However, once people step onto the American soil, a different vibe takes place altogether. Some of us begin to suffer. Some of us begin to drown in uncertainty. Feeling overwhelmed by negative thoughts, we lose our sense of direction and forget how to live meaningfully or achieve the dreams deeply embedded in our core.

Like myself, some of us go through the routine motions of everyday life, craving change, yet we suffer from feeling unfulfilled. For more than ten years, I have been searching, asking, and learning about personal change and transformation. I wanted to be the person that Allah created me to be, but I had no idea where to begin, or who that person was even supposed to be. I had the same burning questions and concerns like many of you, desiring and wanting to change, but I didn't know how to do it. I realized that all change begins with one's mindset. Once my mindset was corrected, things began to change for the better.

When I was about twelve years old, I used to ask my family members and other Muslim people whom I thought would have the answers to my questions, "What is the purpose of life?" It turned out that even Muslim adults didn't know the answer to this question, or maybe they did, and did not know how articulate it to me. Then, when I would ask them, "Is there a God?" they would get angry, because apparently I should have known not to ask such questions, and I should have known the answer already.

As an Afghani Muslim, my history is rooted in Islam and Islamic scholarship, so to question the existence of God, which is the foundation of the Afghani people, was unheard of. You see, dismissing my questions didn't help me. It only caused me to think that Islam didn't have the answers I was looking for. To this end, I began to seek answers in other religions and philosophies. I looked into the world's major religions and I couldn't agree either with their books, eschatology, theology, or faithful praxis.

In 2003, by the grand design of Allah, my mother befriended a woman whose husband was involved with an organization called WhyIslam, and this is the same organization that I have been volunteering with for nearly a decade. As a volunteer with WhyIslam, the brother used to teach non-Muslim people about Islam and by the grace of Allah, dispel misconceptions, and since then, many people embraced Islam through our organization. The brother was extremely intelligent. He was a computer engineer, and gave dawah (called others to Islam), and he was the first person I met who was learning Arabic. He said he wanted to understand the language of the Quran, to know what Allah was saying without needing a translation.

Whenever my family and I would come over to his house, he would make us watch videotapes about the science and miracles of the Quran. What I learned from those tapes fascinated me. He began telling us about the Quran, and he took out one big sturdy Quran with English translation in it, which at the time was too big for my small hands to carry. I asked him if I could have the Quran, and he asked if I would read it, and I promised him that I would. And I did. As I held the Quran in my hands,

I asked him, "What's the purpose of life?" He said that I knew the answer, and refused to tell me. I had no idea what he was talking about. I almost begged him to tell me, but he said I had to figure it out on my own, because I already knew the answer. It was frustrating to the say the least.

For the next three years, I learned about the major religions of the world. Whenever I found what I felt to be a flaw in the concept of God or in any necessary aspects of a certain religion, I became disinterested. I wandered from one ideology to another, and none of them made sense to me. Those were some of the most difficult and painful years I have ever endured, because it hurt not knowing who Allah was. I had sort of become an agnostic, and continued my search for the Creator.

What is strange to me and until this day I cannot fully comprehend the reasons behind it is that I never stopped praying or fasting and I continued to read the Quran during that time. I think I knew that I would feel empty if I stopped doing those deeds. Listening to the Quran used to make my eyes well up with tears, and it made my heart happy and at peace for reasons I could not fully understand at the time. I found the recitation of Quran so heavy upon me that I used to feel its weight pushing me down into prostration. I still feel this way until today.

Also, whenever I used to read it, I understood what tranquility and peace felt like and I never wanted those feelings to dissipate. Having experienced all of this, some people might wonder how it is possible to worship Allah and still not be sure of the purpose of life, or if there was even a God. I think that I have always believed in Allah, but I think what I was looking for was proof of His existence. I had also been looking for a step-by-step guideline of what I was supposed to do with my life, but I did not find such a guideline in the Quran that told me what I needed to do from A to Z, nor did anyone teach it to me. I was left to continue my search and wonder about the Creator.

I had always been fascinated by the perfection of creation, and how it all came to be, but during my search, my curiosity only peaked more and more in my insatiable need to understand the creation, and thus, understand life. I wondered about the sky, the trees, the universe, black holes, planets, and the human beings, and our thoughts. Where did thoughts come from? It only made sense that all of these beautiful creations would have a Creator, because they didn't create themselves. But who did?

One day when I was about fifteen years old, I sat on the green hill in the park near my house. I was tired, confused, uncertain, and even sad, because it had been too long since I had been wondering about the Creator, and I still did not know if He existed or not. I looked up at the sky, and the trees and I was truly amazed by their creation. In fact, everything about creation fascinated me, even things that people overlooked or didn't necessarily see as beautiful like gray roads, or even dirt. This is because I always wondered about their origins, their Creator. All of this lead me to think that there had to be a Creator, but I still needed one final push.

While I sat there on the hill, I looked to the left of me, and I saw a pile of sand. At first, I didn't see it, but as I looked at it more, I saw a microscopic little insect moving on top of it. I scooped up the sand underneath it in my palm, and stared at this sand-colored creature that was now moving in my hand. In my fascination with the existence of this creature, I said, "What are *you* doing in this world?"

Then I knew. I knew that there had to be a Creator. Everything was too perfect and none of it could have happened on its own as some of my atheist friends claimed or that we came from apes. I knew that for a creature so tiny and so seemingly insignificant that could have been easily crushed by merely blowing on it, there had to be a reason why it existed and why the world and I existed. That day was one of the happiest days of my life.

Now, all I had to figure out was, "What is the purpose of life?" I turned to the Quran. I knew that the Quran had to be the true book of guidance because of my own experiences with it, and the miracles and science in it that I had learned a few years earlier. Soon after, as I read the Quran, the purpose of life became clear to me. One day when I opened up the Quran, I read what I had been searching for all those aching years. Allah said, "And I have not created the Jinn and mankind except to worship Me," (51:56). It was so clear. We were here on this earth to worship Allah. It was so simple.

You can't imagine my happiness and relief after coupling these two facts together of the existence of Allah and realizing that the purpose of life was to worship Him. You might have seen a new Muslim cry immediately after having accepted Islam; I know what that feels like. Fortunate are the ones who don't ever have to live a moment without knowing who Allah is.

After the realization that Allah was the Creator, and that I was supposed to worship Him, the existence of the universe made sense to me. My own life made sense to me. I realized that the brother from WhyIslam was right—I did know the purpose of life. It was right there in front of me all along. Allah's existence made my world not just okay, but it made me grateful and optimistic. I couldn't believe that someone as insignificant as I had even been a thought to Allah. Al-Khaliq (The Creator) became one of my most favorite names of Allah ever since then, because without the Creator, nothing makes sense.

From that moment forward, my mindset changed, and it became rooted in Islamic principles of hope, positivity, optimism, and always expecting the best from Allah. This is when I first encountered the Muslim mindset. My uncertainty and confusion that had followed me around like a shadow for years finally dissipated. My self-transformation began as I was finally lead to the realization of Allah's existence and knowing that Islam was a true religion. I then began my journey to follow and adopt Islam wholeheartedly as my way of life. I decided that I would try to learn what Allah wanted from me in the Quran, even if it took a lifetime. By setting out on the journey of learning, I continued striving towards the betterment of my thoughts and my view of the world. My purpose in this life became clear and working daily towards having a better mindset has been tremendously helpful in attaining meaning and remaining optimistic no matter what, and I want the same for you.

Through research, studying, and my own experiences, I have compiled this book for all of you who are going through what I went through of being lost in uncertainty and feeling like you just don't know what to do.

To all Muslim brothers and sisters who don't know where to begin, but know that they want to be better today than they were yesterday, this book is for you. For any Muslim struggling with personal change, this book will help point you in the right direction and show you practical steps in achieving your goals inshallah. God willing.

I have personally tried and tested the concepts I talk about in this book. I have found that which leads to fulfillment, and so can you.

If you implement the guidelines on a daily basis and/or regularly, you will achieve a positive mindset and forge ahead into the future with confidence and direction.

Don't be the person who continues to live in uncertainty and negativity for even one more day. Don't be the person who merely wishes and dreams to be accomplished one day.

Be the kind of person who, all the while knowing that Allah is in control, takes control of his or her life. Be the kind of person whom people will want to follow and emulate, all the way to Jannah inshallah. Take action, and do so immediately.

Determine your own legacy by taking the first step today. Decide now that you will no longer accept mediocrity and anxiety as a lifestyle and do so by achieving a positive mindset, a Muslim mindset.

Take action by reading *The Muslim Mindset* today and design an extraordinary life for yourself, and then help others along the way inshallah.

You will love the new life you are on your way to creating inshallah, so keep reading and striving on your journey to architecting a beautiful life, full of meaning, optimism, and excitement.

This book is for you if you are tired of being tired, feeling stuck, and being stagnant. If you want to be more, achieve more, but don't know where to begin, then this is a place where you can start. This book gives you the tools, tips, and tricks to take inventory of your own life, and arrive at practical solutions and steps to help you decide what you want more of or less of in your thoughts, actions, relationships, and goals. This book also teaches you prophetic practices with supporting evidences from the Quran, the Prophet Mohammad, peace be upon him, some of his companions, may Allah be pleased with them, and other pious scholars, and teachers I have known in my own life whose knowledge and practices will help you, God willing, with achieving a positive mental attitude in your everyday life as a Muslim.

The Muslim Mindset has been designed to help guide you in making that change become a reality, and to achieve anything through a positive mindset while being a practicing Muslim.

Throughout the rest of the book, you will find guidelines that will walk you through the process of achieving a Muslim mindset. I do caution you not to expect results in one day. Although you may experience positivity and optimism, it requires more time and effort for your mindset to shift from a negative to a positive one and for it to become a state that you are almost always in. However, it is duly doable even for the faintest of hearts.

What is the Muslim Mindset?

ANY positive change begins in the mind. In order for our lives to change for the better and transform, we have to transform our mindsets. We have to believe that Allah has bestowed upon us the gifts and abilities to achieve what we need to and want to in life. This is a mindset. Your pattern of beliefs displayed over a certain period of time is a mindset.

We want to make sure that the mindset we attain is a positive one. In order to have a positive mindset, according to psychologist Dr. Carol Dweck, we must believe that our ability to change and improve is malleable, that it is not fixed, and that, if we want to, we can change at any moment in our lives through effort, training and practice. If we are struggling today, we can correct our mindset; we will know that it is not the end of the world, and that we can become better with

persistent practice, consistency, ⸺
don't necessarily rely on how sma
we place emphasis on our ability to
every single day.

A negative mindset is exactly the opposite. Dr. Dweck calls it the "fixed mindset." In this type of mindset, people believe that the abilities they have been given are not changeable, and cannot be improved. They are often afraid of failure, and fear looking unintelligent, so they avoid taking on new endeavors or improving their thoughts and skills. If we study the lives of the companions of the Prophet Mohammad, peace be upon him, and the lives of our pious predecessors, we will realize that Islam might not have gotten very far if they had avoided taking on the incredible challenge of adopting an entire new way of life. They took risks, even at the expense of looking unintelligent or crazy to others around them.

A negative mindset focuses on problems and usually expects the worst possible scenario in almost every situation. A negative mindset is pessimistic, untrusting of others, and gives up without much effort. People with a negative mindset are often stressed, anxious, and experience a deep sadness. They are also usually alone, have terrible health problems, and see the world as a gloomy and boring place to live in. They also usually attract negative others to themselves.

They are often ungrateful and impatient, complaining and underestimating their own abilities and gifts that are bestowed upon them by Allah. They expect the worst to happen to them, and it usually does, which only further perpetuates their negative view of themselves and of the world. This is the kind of mindset we need to avoid, and work towards a positive mindset, or the Muslim mindset.

It is possible to achieve a positive mindset or a belief and worldview that leads to phenomenal changes as seen in the lives of the companions of Prophet Mohammad, peace be upon him, and the pious predecessors. A mindset that is rooted in Islamic principles such as hope, optimism, thinking positive, always looking for the best in every situation, being grateful, remaining patient during difficulties and putting one's trust in Allah is a Muslim mindset. This kind of mindset is a lens through which the believer filters out negativity and allows for growth, healing, and acceptance of life as it is while being aware that Allah has given him or her the ability to live a fulfilling and meaningful life. Therefore, the believer recognizes that Allah has given him a certain level of control and free will to make life the way he or she wants it to be. Thus, negativity falls by the wayside, and optimism permeates the believer's world no matter how bleak circumstances may seem, and this mainly stems from the most important aspect of life, which is to have belief in Allah and trust in His plans for you, and thus, a Muslim mindset.

One of the greatest, perhaps *the greatest* boxer of all times, Muhammad Ali (may Allah have mercy upon him), was one of the best examples of people who had an extraordinary mindset. According to Dr. Dweck, "Boxing experts relied on physical measurements, called 'tales of the tapes,' to identify naturals. They included measurements of the fighter's fist, reach, chest expansion and weight. Muhammad Ali failed these measurements. He was not a natural. He had great speed, but he didn't have the physique of a great fighter, he didn't have the strength, and he didn't have the classical moves. In fact, he boxed all wrong." Then Dr. Dweck wrote, "But aside from his quickness, Ali's brilliance was his mind." It has been said about Muhammad Ali by a famous boxing manager that "'He was a paradox. His physical performances in the ring were absolutely wrong… Yet, his brain was in perfect working condition.' 'He showed us all,' he continued with a broad smile across his face, 'that all victories come from here,' hitting his forehead with his index finger. Then he raised a pair of fists, saying: 'Not from here.'" Muhammad Ali is one of the best examples of people who fought against all odds because of his mindset.

A Muslim mindset is positive in nature. This is a state in which a believer expects optimistic and positive results in every obstacle, challenge, and facet of life just like Muhammad Ali did, even though he was not what a typical boxer looked like. A Muslim mindset is the persistence of one's focus on optimistic thoughts in his or her beliefs, health, finances, and relationships. It is a mindset in which we see the world through the lens of Islam. It is a paradigm, or view, through which we decipher life by emulating the Prophet Mohammad, peace be upon him, his companions, our pious predecessors, and implementing their methods in the way one lives. We strive to emulate their lives in the worship of Allah, finding inner peace and purpose in life, building and maintaining healthy relationships and good health, and in living in hope and positivity. Through the Muslim mindset, we filter out the good and focus on it, remaining grateful to Allah, and coping with challenges in life in a healthy manner.

A Muslim mindset is important to achieve, especially in times of difficulties. It is a "mental toughness," as Dr. Dweck writes. It is the ability to withstand hardships and keep going, even if the tide is not in your favor. Everyone goes through adversity. No religion, culture, people, or ethnicities are free of hardships. We all experience bad days. We all experience crises and life's most toughest and devastating hardships that cause us to have a whirl of emotions, often times, negative ones.

What is important is how we handle these hardships and what we do about them. Therefore, our mindset is the key to handling all of life's problems, difficulties, hardships, and even traumas. We have been given the tools, abilities, and resources to handle all of life's difficulties and struggles. You have the solutions to your problems, and its secrets lie in your mindset.

By adopting the Muslim mindset, a believer can face challenges head on, remain patient, and have full conviction in the deepest parts of his heart that Allah will always be there for him. Our mindset is the key to all success that one achieves in this life and in the hereafter. As Muslims, we are taught from a young age to think well of Allah and to always expect good from Him. As narrated in Riyad Al-Saliheen, the Prophet, peace be upon him said, "Allah, the Exalted said, 'I am as My servant thinks I am (expects me to be). I am with him when he mentions Me. If he mentions Me to himself, I mention him to Myself; and if he mentions Me in an assembly, I mention him in an assembly greater than it (the gathering of the angels). If he draws near to Me a hand's length, I draw near to him an arm's length. And if he comes to me walking, I go to him running."

This positive view of Allah is a Muslim mindset. The more we think well of Allah, the more we receive. This is the nature of life. It is law. Our expectations of Allah must be rooted in optimism and hope. We have to think that Allah will come to us running if we ever need anything. We are never alone, because Allah is always watching us and caring for us.

The companion of the Prophet Mohammad, peace be upon him, Ibn Masud (may Allah be pleased with him) said, "I swear by the one who there is nothing worthy of worship except Him, no one thinks about Allah a thought, except that Allah gives him what he thinks, and all of that is good in the hands of Allah."[1] Allah, too, says in the Quran, "Then what is your thought about the Lord of the worlds?"[2] These are but only a few narrations and verses of the many more that illustrate the necessity of a correct Muslim mindset, thinking, and having positive thoughts, opinions, and expectations of Allah. All virtues are in the hands of Allah, and we can be its beneficiaries by modeling and practicing Islamic principles of the right mindset.

Throughout the rest of the book, I will outline the guidelines of how to achieve a Muslim mindset

---

[1] Muhsin, Shaykh Abdur Razzaaq ibn Abdul, "Having Good Thoughts About Allah," *AbdurRahman.org,* 20 Apr, 2014, Web, 6 July, 2017.
[2] 37:87

inshallah, God willing. Although there are many ways and paths to do this, I have included ten lessons that I think will be most beneficial in achieving such a mindset. Each lesson contains practical tricks, tips and solutions to help make its implementation in our day-to-day lives easy. If you take away nothing else from this book, at least take away this: Allah is to you as you think of Him. So, go to Him walking, and He will come to you running.

Lesson 1:
Increase Your Eman

FOR a believer, the most important and life-altering decision one has to make in order to achieve a Muslim mindset is to have faith in Allah, our Creator. In other words, he or she must have eman. Both worlds of the Muslim—the world in which we currently live, and the hereafter, which we will live in after our death—depend upon eman.

Our eman has a direct effect on our realities in both worlds. Therefore, if we desire a good outcome for ourselves, our families, and our communities, we need to work on increasing, and strengthening our eman, which can be attained through the implementation of various Islamic practices such as seeking knowledge, fulfilling the obligatory acts, reciting the Qur'an, remembering death, and remembering Allah. When we achieve a status of eman in which we feel attached to Allah, and we feel it would hurt too much to separate from Him, we will notice our mindsets shifting from negativity and/or indifference towards positivity and optimism.

What is eman? The scholars say that eman is the action of the heart, meaning to affirm faith and belief in Allah in your heart. Then it is to affirm it with your tongue, and to follow it with action of the limbs.[3] In this chapter, all three components of eman have been included so that we can hopefully strengthen it by the permission of Allah.

Eman is affirming the existence of Allah, to know that there is a single Creator without any partner. He is at all times watching over us, guiding us, and providing for us. He is the one who gives life and takes it away as well. To Allah is our final return.

Eman is also to affirm the creation of Allah like the angels. It is to affirm that they are the noble servants of Allah, and they do not disobey Him in what He has commanded them. They are created from light, and do not eat or drink. We do not describe them as males or females and we do not say that they are given birth to or that they give birth. We don't know how many of them there are, because only Allah knows their count.[4] Eman is

---

[3] Dr. Al-Bugha, Mostafa. *Al-Wafa.* (Beirut: Dar ibn Kathir, 2003). Print. 15.
[4] Dr. Al-Bugha, 15.

also to believe in the books and scriptures that Allah has sent. These scriptures include the scrolls given to Ibrahim, the Psalms given to Dawood, the Torah given to Musa, the New Testament given to Esa, and the Quran given to Mohammad, peace be upon them all. We also must affirm our belief in all of the messengers and prophets of Allah who were sent to guide us back to Allah. Eman also requires believing in the Day of Judgment, because we will be resurrected on this day and asked about our deeds. The final parts of eman are to believe that Allah has given us freewill, which is paramount to this book, and to also believe in predestination—that some things are preordained for us like who our parents are. All of these actions include the heart, the tongue, and the limbs, and are included throughout the rest of this lesson and book.

I believe that having faith in Allah is so powerful and so important that even if one was starving or suffering from the most heinous atrocities, his faith would not waver in the least. Knowing that Allah exists allows us as Muslims to place our trust in Him, even if we were faced with difficulties and/or problems that might otherwise cause us to have worries, anxiety, and even depression. We recognize that Allah is the one who removes all pain and He is the one who heals all hearts, and so we remain patient until His help and aid reach us.

I don't want us to misunderstand an important fact here about going through pain as Muslims, and it is that we are not indifferent to it. As Muslims, we do experience pain, hardships, uncertainty, grief, worries and possibly even depression, and if we experience any of these or possibly even more than this, it does not make any of us *less* of a Muslim. There are many examples of pain, suffering and hardships that prophets, the companions, and even the pious generations have endured, and we cannot say that because they cried or felt pain that they had no eman or that their eman was weak. In the Quran, we learn of one of the most heartbreaking stories of Prophet Ayoub, peace be upon him, who suffered pain, loss and disease for eighteen years and yet his faith in Allah remained strong. Pain, adversity and suffering are a natural part of life. It is normal. What makes it easier to endure it is our faith in Allah, and placing our trust in Him.

Recognizing and learning about who Allah is, is vital to our lives on this earth. As believers, it is our duty and our only mission in life to know Allah and worship Him. Nothing else matters. But you see, this too is a mindset. You can cultivate such a mindset and live a life so empowered and so sure that even if the sky were to fall apart, it would not even faze you in the least. This is a result of one's belief in the existence of Allah, knowing that He is there and will not let any harm come to us.

Allah's existence makes everything okay. No problem, difficulty, or hardship matters as long as Allah exists, and He will exist forever. He is eternal. So what does that tell you? It means that at any point in time, or space, nothing matters other than Allah. His existence and gaining His pleasure is all that is important. We don't even matter, although Allah loves the creation of the human beings.

So, how can we make sure we believe and have eman in such a way that Allah becomes the center of our focus and our life? Below, I have some guidelines to help increase and strengthen our eman, so we will never be too worried again by anything in life, and we can live optimistically and positively inshallah.

Seek Knowledge

The first step in increasing and strengthening our eman is that we must learn about who Allah is, and what He, the Most Compassionate, requires of us. We believe in Him and want to worship Him, but many of us lack the knowledge of how to do so. Therefore, seeking knowledge is one of the best actions we can take to draw nearer to Allah, and strengthen our eman. The Prophet Mohammad, peace be upon him, said, "To seek sacred knowledge is an obligation upon every Muslim."[5] Abdur-Rahman ibn Yusuf explains in his commentary of this narration that every Muslim must seek as much religious knowledge as will suffice him in fulfilling the obligatory acts of worship. In Riyad Al-Saliheen, we also learn the importance of seeking knowledge, and it is that the Prophet Mohammad, peace be upon him, said, "Whoever Allah wants good for, He gives him an understanding of the religion." We learn from this hadith that when people seek knowledge, they are guided by Allah to pursue such endeavors. They are chosen by Allah to seek knowledge, and to have an understanding of Islam.

We should pray to Allah to make us of those who are given an understanding of the religion. We should make it a daily habit to ask Allah for knowledge and guidance. Allah will surely fulfill our requests and provide for us from where we never thought possible. However, it matters where and whom we get our knowledge from.

Seek knowledge from a trusted scholar in your community. Inquire about Islamic classes in your local masjid. If you do not have a masjid nearby, and it would be too difficult to go to ones further away, ask your masjid's leadership, scholar, or

---

[5] Al-Bulandshehri, Shaykh Ashiq Ilahi, *Provisions for the Seekers,* trans. Ibn Yusuf, Abdur-Rahman (Santa Barbara: White Thread Press, 2009), 41.

imam about having online classes with the community. Keep it simple. My family and I used to have a sheikh call our house on the phone and we would put it on speaker while he gave a lecture. Slowly, we invited other community women to join and listen to his talk.

There are also free classes on websites dedicated to teaching Muslims about Islam like Seeker's Hub, which is run by the respected Shaykh Faraz Rabbani. Ask the trusted scholars in your community about websites and resources that are available for seeking knowledge.

The objective here is not to make excuses for our selves. There are many resources available to us in America that other people in some other countries may not have access to. So, ask Allah and do your part. Allah will open doors for you to gain knowledge and get to know Him and His religion. Inshallah, once you start the path to seeking knowledge, you will never quench your thirst. You will only want to learn more and more inshallah.

Fulfill the Obligatory Acts

Perform all the obligatory acts (fard & wajib) to the best of your ability, which are mainly the action of the limbs. As Muslims, it is difficult to feel good about ourselves and to have a positive mindset if we are not fulfilling Allah's commandments.

It is natural for human beings to have a desire for connecting with Allah, but we cannot be connected to Him if we break the chain that connects us. This means that we should pray our five daily prayers on time and in the correct manner. We must train ourselves to focus in salah (prayer) and have sincerity.

I recognize that this is easier said than done, but really, all Allah wants us to do is our part. As for the rest, He will take care of it for us inshallah.

My Arabic teacher narrated to us a story of a man who prayed for twenty years, and never felt any connection to Allah, or change in his heart. However, he continued to pray without delay. Then for the next twenty years, he felt the sweetness of salah. The objective here is to fulfill and uphold the commandments of Allah, whether we feel like it or not. Strive for sincerity in your prayers, whether you accomplish it or not. Allah will respond to you, and He will make it easy for you, but we must put in the effort first.

We cannot expect Allah to just suddenly transform our prayers, and our lives overnight, although it is not hard for Him to do that. Life is a long process, so we need to make sure that we adopt the practice of regularly enjoining the commandments in the way they have been prescribed, and do so sincerely. Then, similar to the man who prayed for twenty years, we can also taste the sweetness of not only salah, but the sweetness and serenity of every act of worship we do inshallah.

Keep in mind that when we are connected to Allah in salah, we automatically feel better for the rest of the day. You will feel a boost in your satisfaction with your prayer and feel at ease. This feeling is from Allah and a direct result of your prayer being done with excellence. It is also the result of recitation.

I believe that our prayers are what really define us as people and define our status with Allah. Prayer is what keeps us away from sins and shamelessness, strengthens our eman, and contributes to our spiritual, mental, and emotional wellbeing. Therefore, if you find yourself in difficulties, one of the personal things to analyze is your salah, and all of us should work on making it better.

It has been said that whenever our beloved Prophet Mohammad, peace be always upon him, was afflicted with difficulty, he would rush to salah. Prayer is the solution. It is a direct link to the Creator of the heavens and the earth.

Fulfill all obligatory acts of worship. Give zakat if you meet the qualifications, fast during the month of Ramadan, and go to Hajj, the pilgrimage.

These acts are the most beloved to Allah of all the other acts, starting with affirming that Allah is one, and that Muhammad, peace be upon him, is the final messenger of Allah.

Another commandment that some do not realize is a very big part of Islam is the wearing of the head covering, the hijab, for sisters.

Every day that a sister chooses to let a person (who is not allowed to) see her hair, she is considered sinful. Sins deplete barakah or blessings from one's life. We may be pursuing great endeavors and we may be actively involved in contributing positively to our communities through volunteering and helping those who have less than us, but that is not what is immediately obligatory upon us. Inshallah, we should fulfill the commandments first and everything that is extra or just nice to do, we can do afterwards.

Some Muslim sisters are deterred from wearing hijab, because they think that they are not pious enough to represent what the hijab means. I can completely relate to this and understand why someone might think that way. By nature, human beings are good people and crave authenticity, so they may not want to wear the hijab, because they think that their inner state would be incongruent with their outer appearance. This thought process of not wanting to seem hypocritical, or phony, stems from a beautiful place; however, it is a misunderstanding about the hijab. Allah did not make it a condition that we had to be perfect human beings before we could outwardly represent His religion and His commandments. Allah already knows that we are flawed and sinful human beings, and yet He still mandated that we wear hijab and cover up.

Talk to the scholars in your community if you have difficulty wearing the hijab or if you would simply like to know more. Inshallah they can help us learn more about this topic, and they are so kind mashallah that they always offer words of encouragement and wisdom. We should not delay getting closer to Allah, and we can achieve closeness to Him by following His commandments.

The hijab is a distinction between Muslims and non-Muslims. It is an honor for a woman to be covered up and protected from all that could harm her. It is an elevation of her status, and it is a means of getting closer to Allah and attaining His pleasure.

Just as the hijab is an honor and a cause for distinction amongst Muslims and non-Muslims, it can be argued that the beard serves a similar purpose for brothers as well. I understand that currently there is a trend going on where even the non-Muslims are allowing their beards to grow; therefore, some might argue that brothers cannot be distinguished from non-Muslim men. As I mentioned, it is just a trend. It will go away and be replaced by another trend as is the nature of trends. However, Muslim brothers always have beards, and they can be recognized as Muslims, and they should be proud, and this positively impacts our mindset.

However, one might ask, "What does the hijab have to with achieving a positive mindset?" The reason I mention the hijab, which includes dressing in an Islamic manner and behaving well as best as we can, is that because it is sinful, it affects one's mindset. It may go unnoticed at first, but as time goes on, it becomes more apparent.

Sins decrease barakah in our day-to-day lives, and this can also affect our attitude, our emotions, our views of ourselves, and the world. Therefore, it behooves us to make our lives as sinless as possible, so we can feel that we have drawn closer to Allah and fill our lives with blessings. As we draw closer to Allah, we feel at peace, content, blessed, optimistic, grateful, and happy.

The more prophetic practices we make a part of our lives, the more blessings we attain, which can help us live optimistically and live life in a way that is pleasing and beloved to Allah. Ask Allah to make it easy for you to wear a proper hijab and not fear its consequences. Ask Allah to grant you the strength to have a beard and not fear its consequences.

To reiterate, what we need to do first is fulfill the daily commandments required of us like the prayers, fasting in Ramadan, giving charity (zakat), going to hajj (the pilgrimage to Mecca), and wearing hijab for women. Inshallah, through the fulfillment of the obligatory acts, we can achieve a Muslim mindset.

Recite Quran Daily

The recitation of the Quran is vital in achieving a Muslim mindset. Although this is an action of the tongue, it has profound effects on your heart, which makes it an action of the heart as well. As Muslims, we need to make the recitation of the Quran a daily habit.

Recite for even fifteen minutes a day at the time of Fajr (dawn prayer), and automatically, you will feel accomplished, happier, and more energetic. As you continue this practice, it will become easier for you.

Stay consistent, because the most beloved deeds to Allah are those that are consistent, even if they are small.[6] Before you begin the recitation of the Quran, have wudhu or ablution, which is the washing of the face, limbs, and wiping over the

---

[6] Al-Bulandshehri, 42

head. Have the intention in your heart that you are only reciting it for the sake of Allah.

Keep in mind that you are receiving reward for every letter that you recite. Allah grants you ten rewards for every letter you recite inshallah. Remember that you are reciting the words of the Creator, Allah.

Reciting the Quran seems like a small, and insignificant task, because we expect big insurmountable feats when we think of achieving a positive mindset or accomplishing major goals. However, it is exactly the opposite. You must remember that you are doing a beloved deed that the Prophet Mohammad, peace be upon him, used to do, and He is the best of creation. If he, peace be upon him, did this, then we should without a doubt make it a regular habit and excel in its practice. The prophet Mohammad, peace be upon him, said, "The best among you is he who learns the Quran and teaches it."[7]

As you continue this habit daily inshallah, it will have a compounding effect. What do I mean by that?

The compound effect means that as you continue to do a certain activity or think a certain thought, it will add up over time to a big outcome. For example, as you continue to recite the Quran,

---

[7] Al-Bulandshehri, 42

even for ten minutes a day, it will become easier for you to read for longer periods of time through the progression of time. You might even begin to read more often during the day. For example, instead of just reading in the morning, you will also want to read in the evening as well as after every salah. You might begin to read a whole juz (a whole section) per day and begin to finish the Quran monthly inshallah.

The compounding effect is also witnessed in other aspects of your life. For example, the recitation of the Quran might make it easier for you to do other acts of worship that were not in your habit before. You might begin to memorize the Quran or begin to fast voluntarily due to the blessings bestowed upon you because of your recitation. It may increase love and peace between your family members, or you might be able to get your work done faster in a shorter span of time.

Many compounding good things can happen as a result of your recitation of the Quran. This is because when you recite the Quran, especially at Fajr, the angels descend and witness your recitation. They love that you recite the Quran, so you are never alone.

As the angels descend upon you, so do blessings. As your house becomes filled with blessings, it leads to the compounding effect of being able to achieve other good deeds, in an even shorter amount of time. Your time will be filled with blessings, and that is why you can do many other good deeds.

The blessings that descend upon you and fill your house have an effect on your heart. It will encourage you to have a positive mental attitude and maintain a positive mindset.

Remember Death

Death is an uncomfortable thought for many. It is not something most people even like to discuss, because then they would realize that they are not living in this world forever.

However, no matter how uncomfortable and terrifying the idea of death is, we have to accept it, because it will happen. As Muslims, we are taught from a young age to prepare for our death. The gift for the believer is death, because it is what stands between him and Allah, and it is only after his death that he will meet Allah.[8]

However, many people are heedless of the meeting with Allah and focus their attention on worldly acquisitions to such an extent that they live in denial about death. Come to terms with death. Learn about it and begin to prepare for it inshallah.

---

[8] Al-Bulandshehri, 47

Inquire from within. Usually, you have most of the answers inside your heart, and if you don't have a certain answer, Allah has made all the resources available for you to find out. Ask yourself,

What would I do if I had one year to live?

What would I do if I had only six months to live?

What would I do if I had one day to live?

Now, really think about this. If you are doing now what you would be doing if you had a year, six months, or even one day to live, then that's incredible. If, however, you are not, then ask yourself, "Why not?" Even if we are doing what we would be doing in our last moments, we can always improve, so look for ways of how you can do that. Other than Allah, you know yourself best.

As we accept the reality of death, and realize that our life is temporary, that which is important in our lives becomes clear. Life is transitory, and very soon all of us will face that reality.

When you think about how it is that you would like to live, write it all down in a list. Pick three to five items from the list that are most important to you and begin working towards them immediately.

When you remember death, especially when you are facing difficulties, look at that day or experience as though it were your last day. If we look at difficulties or life in general, with the thought in mind that we may not have much time to live, suddenly the problem becomes minute and even irrelevant. We will accept reality and not be bothered by it, because we have bigger goals and thoughts in mind. We, Muslims, don't allow it to bother or frustrate us because Allah exists, and we surrender ourselves to His Will wholly.

Whatever happens, let it be. Leave all of your affairs, difficulties, and helplessness to Allah. Allah will take care of it for you. Allah created you and wants good for you. As long as you have Allah, you have everything.

This type of thought process will help make it easier to overcome difficulties, have patience, and prevent overwhelming our selves. It leads to a broader perspective of life as a whole and makes it easier to achieve peace of mind and live meaningfully. May Allah accept our good deeds and make the journey of transformation towards Him easy, starting with a positive mindset inshallah.

Be Alone with Allah

Set up a time daily for solitude with Allah. It can be a few minutes to an hour. Sit in a quiet place, preferably in your prayer room where you are completely alone with Allah, without any noise or distractions.

Use this alone time to think about your life, your purpose, and the difficulties you are facing, if any.

Are you living the life you really want?

Are you living life the way you were meant to live it?

The objective of a believer is not that he has happiness and money in this life. Rather, we are striving towards excellence in our thoughts and intentions so that our deeds become acceptable to Allah, and even if we were the poorest in this world, we would be of the most fortunate in the hereafter, and we would be of those with the richest of hearts.

This book is not about finding happiness in this life, although it can do that for you. It is about seeking holiness and whole-y-ness. We are striving towards becoming whole and achieving excellence in our deeds and character, which includes our mindset.

During your time of solitude with Allah, think about His all-encompassing mercy, His Greatness, Power, and Supremeness. He is Allah. He is the one who has control and power over every leaf that falls and every grain of sand that is turned. He is Allah who controls every heartbeat of yours and forgives every sin.

Praise Allah with all of His beautiful names and attributes. Praise His prophets, especially our final Messenger, peace be upon him. This is an action of the tongue, which will also affect your heart.

Know that hope exists for you too. Allah will provide a way out for you out of every difficulty and provide for you from where you could have never imagined. That is His promise to His servants.[9] Allah has made it incumbent upon Himself to provide for us. Glory be to Him. What kind of a being makes it incumbent and necessary upon Himself to provide? How magnificent He is! So rely upon Allah, because He is sufficient for you.

Use this alone time with Allah to cry to Him for guidance, forgiveness, and mercy. Use this time to seek clarity and blessings in every aspect of your life. Although we cannot attain complete certainty, because that is the nature of life and there exist things of the unseen, which we have no knowledge of, pray for what is possible of certainty in your own life.

During your solitude with Allah, think about your days or many days and months. Did you really complete every action you were supposed to take with complete devotion, attention, concentration, and excellence?

---

[9] Quran 65:3

If not, which is the case for many of us, then why not? What prevented you from completing each act with excellence? Write it all down and begin by working on improving one at a time. Remove the things that hinder you from excelling in your worship and in having positive thoughts. Do your best to avoid obstacles or distractions that take you away from your obligatory acts of worship, and be sure to check back in with your list to look at your progress.

I believe life is an accumulation of the choices we make. This time of solitude with Allah is perfect for reflecting about the choices we have made and the patterns we have carved out that we have been stuck in for so long. It is time to break out of this perpetual cycle of negativity and stagnancy and seriously focus on how we choose to spend the rest of our days on this earth.

What is beautiful about life is that Allah will give you whatever you want. Pause and think about that for a moment. *Allah will give you whatever you want.*

If you want a life of ease, Allah will give it to you. If you want a life of abundance, peace, meaning, and health, He will also give it to you. So, if Allah never rejects any of our duas, why would we not ask for the best of the best in both worlds?

Some people have the misconception that we should not ask Allah for the good of this world, and that we should only make dua for the hereafter. Although asking for the best of the akhira is better, we should still ask for this life as well. Allah does not tire of your asking, in fact, it makes Him happy.

How strange is it that when you keep asking and nagging Allah, it makes Him happy, and you become more beloved to Him, and yet when you ask of people, not even nagging, they become annoyed of you and distance themselves from you.

So, ask of Allah, and ask Him for the abundance of both worlds, an abundance of that which is most meaningful to you, and most beloved to Him, The Exalted.

During your time of solitude, do prophetic dhikr, which is the remembrance of Allah. Make duas that Prophet Mohammad, peace be upon him, used to make. Dhikr strengthens your memory, causes blessings to descend upon you, and you become protected from any evil or unfortunate event that might befall you.

Dhikr blesses your time, so you are able to accomplish more than you ever could before. Dhikr helps you manage time well so you don't end up wasting any of it while accomplishing your goals.

Keep practicing this act of solitude with Allah, even for just a few minutes a day, and you will notice feeling relieved and worry-free. Inshallah it will make the process of attaining a positive mindset easy for the rest of your days to come.

In conclusion, to embark upon the journey of attaining a Muslim mindset, we must have faith in Allah, or be a person who has eman. As discussed, eman can be strengthened by seeking knowledge, fulfilling the obligatory acts of worship, thinking about the hereafter and preparing for it as well as implementing the regular practice of the recitation of Quran and remembrance of Allah. In turn, we should feel closer to Allah, and hopefully, attain a mindset that is in line with Islam and its tenets of hope, and positivity.

Lesson 2:
Lower Your Wings of Humility for Your Parents

FROM my own experiences, I have learned that my mindset has been very much influenced by my parents. They helped shape the paradigm through which I view the world, and they have helped me continue on my journey to the Muslim mindset. From my parents, I learned about always having hope, even when it seems like there is no way out. I learned from them that we shouldn't complain about life, because there is so much more to be grateful for, and that we must practice kindness and humility no matter what our status is.

In essence, my parents are teachers. They taught me that which is not taught in school, and as a result I have benefited immensely from my relationship with them, especially in the way I see and interact with the world. Just like my parents, everyone else's parents are teachers as well. They are one of the major keys to building our mindsets and influencing us massively for the rest of our lives. It is for this reason that I have dedicated an entire lesson to lowering the wings of humility for our parents, learning from them, and benefitting from them in developing a Muslim mindset, because when our relationships with our parents are positive and in good standing, it will become more easier to achieve a mindset that can help us transform our lives.

I don't think that there is anyone out there who loves you more than your parents; at least, that has been my experience. Nor do I think that there is anyone else out there who sincerely wishes the best for me and seeks nothing in return from me. Most people's parents are the same. So, seek and ask for guidance and support from your parents. If you are having a bad day, or facing some uncertainty in your life, your parents are the best people to go to. Ask them to make dua for you, because Allah never rejects the dua of parents.

I understand some people may not have very good relationships with their parents, and they may find it difficult to talk to them. However, this is the exact reason why it is so necessary to have a great relationship with our parents. Your parents should be your best friends. This type of relationship will grant you wisdom and help you in your present state and in the future. Not only will your parents' wisdom benefit you, it will benefit your children, grandchildren, and generations upon generations to come. They will reap the rewards of your good relationship with your parents and be guided aright inshallah.

The question is, "How do we cultivate such a relationship with our parents?"

People recognize that they probably should have better relationships with their parents, but they often lack the knowledge and wisdom of how to go about achieving that. The first step we must take in strengthening our relationships with our parents is to humble ourselves, to lower our wings of humility. Whoever humbles himself, Allah will elevate him. This is His promise.

Humility is a way to increase our affection and love for our parents, siblings, and even community members. It sews a deep love for you in the hearts of others, and then they will be willing to put you on their heads, and not let your feet touch the ground. They, of their own accord, will elevate you and hold you in high esteem. The question this raises is, "How do we humble ourselves?" The answer to this is simple, yet immensely rewarding when applied in our lives inshallah. We must humble ourselves by acknowledging that our parents have rights over us, and that those rights must be fulfilled. We have a responsibility towards our parents, which means that no matter what the circumstances are, we must always fulfill and uphold their rights upon us. It is a commandment of Allah.

Whatever the case or situation may be, Allah made it mandatory to be dutiful and kind to our parents. So many times in the Quran, directly after calling to His own worship, Allah says to be dutiful to our parents.

We shouldn't even say "uff" to them, or groan, or show our annoyance with them. The Quran, in chapter 17:23-24 says, "Your Rabb has decreed that you worship none but Him, and that you be kind to parents. Whether one or both of them reaches old age in your life, say not to them 'uff,' nor repel them, but address them in terms of honor. And, out of kindness, lower to them the wing of humility, and say: 'My Rabb, bestow upon them mercy as they raised me in childhood.'"

The above verse is referring to old age, but it is applicable to any part of their lives. From this verse, we also learn that we should make dua for our parents and be grateful to Allah, because they raised us when we were little. How strange is it that the time when our parents did the most for us was in our childhood, and yet we don't remember it?

Ibn Kathir, may Allah have mercy upon him, mentions in his book the narration of the Prophet, peace be upon him, who said, "Let him be humbled into dust! Let him be humbled into dust!" Then it was said: "Oh Messenger of Allah, peace be upon him, who is he?" He, peace be upon him, said, "It is he who sees one or both of his parents during their old age, but he does not enter paradise (for he ill-treats them, and does not deal with them kindly and generously)."

The verse and the hadith show how serious it is to neglect our parents or to mistreat them. People who are heedless of their duties towards their parents are looked down upon in Islam, and are subject to incurring Allah's wrath. Therefore, we must extend our generosity, kindness, reverence, and honor to our parents. No harm should reach our parents from us.

We can also humble ourselves by giving them the benefit of doubt, and not dismiss them or their opinions, having already taken the position that we know, and that they do not. We have to be humble enough to know that we don't know everything, and recognize when we need help. We must recognize when we need our *parents*' help. Some problems, especially when we are very young, are too massive for us to handle by ourselves. So ask of them, and they will be more than willing and ready to be of service to you.

Another way to humble ourselves and to cultivate a beautiful relationship with our parents is to allow them to make mistakes, because after all, they are human. We should forgive them for the mistakes they have made even if they did things that concerned you, or even if it made it really difficult to have a mutual respectful relationship with them. Whatever the case is, forgiveness brings about ease and love between people, which will inshallah be addressed a bit later in this book.

We also humble ourselves by recognizing that our parents have lived for years and endured that which we may not ever be able to fathom. Therefore, we respect them, love them, and hold them high above our own heads. Why do I say "above our heads"? It is because the head is the symbol of honor of each individual. If we treat our parents in this way, we make them higher while lowering our own selves, which is a way to humble ourselves.

We must also humble ourselves and not think of our parents as tyrants who rule the kingdom of our households, and think that there is no way to have a decent conversation with them. We shouldn't sell them short and assume that they won't understand our problems, even if they didn't understand them in the past. Instead, we should ask for their opinions and seek their advice and counsel when we are faced with difficulties.

Our parents have years of experience and wisdom that can benefit us today and far into our futures. When you are facing adversity, after turning to Allah, turn to your parents. Their advice and support is always available to us, and they truly have our best interests at heart.

We must humble ourselves in accepting the decisions our parents make and handle it with grace. We should not talk back to them, or even speak about them in a negative way. There is always a reason why they do what they do, which is applicable to anybody. This is why it is so vital to make excuses for people, seventy excuses. By the time you make about five to ten excuses for anyone, you cool off, and empathize with them instead of continuing in your state of negativity and anger.

Therefore, imagine if you could make seventy excuses for them, you might find yourself asking Allah for forgiveness and shedding tears for feeling as though you jumped to conclusions and judged them too quickly without really understanding. You might begin to think about what a difficult life they must have endured and how many hardships they must be facing on a daily basis. I don't think that any of us could even get to seventy excuses, but if, after so many excuses, we still think negatively about them, then we only have ourselves to blame. We are the problem, not them.

Let us not allow ourselves to be so deluded by our perceptions that we fail to understand reality. Not just parents, but most people, are amazing and beautiful. Inshallah Allah gives us the ability and understanding to relate to people in a way that is pleasing to Him, the Most Merciful.

Be easy and mild in temperament with your parents. Be softhearted and kind towards them. Forgive them easily and readily. Let go of the negative experiences you may have had with them, focus on the positive, and reflect and ponder over how much they must have sacrificed for you. Inshallah with this type of attitude towards your parents and others, you will find it much easier to achieve a positive mindset. Allah will help and support you inshallah in your endeavors because He loves that you are kind to your parents, and other people. Allah loves to reward and forgive.

We have now learned the importance of lowering the wing of humility for our parents in achieving a Muslim mindset, because when our relationships with our parents are in good standing, it is much easier to be optimistic and have a solid, and positive foundation. We have also learned how to treat our parents kindly and how to allow room for growth while remaining dutiful towards them. Inshallah if we implement even a few of the ideas discussed in this lesson, we can hopefully gain the pleasure of Allah, and attain a Muslim mindset.

Lesson 3:
Keep Good Company

YOU have most likely heard, "You are who your friends are." This statement is known, and people generally believe it to be true. We are different people with different personalities, habits, and character traits; however, the people whom we choose to associate with ultimately say a lot about who we are and where we might be heading.

Being defined by who your friends are is incredibly profound and filled with wisdom, especially when analyzed and seen through the lens of achieving a Muslim mindset. It is similar to the saying of the Prophet, peace be upon him, when he said, "A person will be with whom he loves."[10] This includes your worldly life and the

---

[10] Al-Bulandshehri, 27.

hereafter, and includes whom you spend your time with.

Our circle of people and friends determines the type of person we are and how we will continue to be in the future. Therefore, it is extremely important to surround yourself with people who can help you draw closer to Allah and to your goals, instead of moving you further away.

What is Good Company?

Good company is made up of those people who remind you about Allah. They encourage you towards doing good, and prevent you or advise you against doing that which would take you away from Allah. They are people who themselves worship Allah, and gaining His pleasure and happiness is their main concern. They are the good company to keep and the best companions to surround our selves with.

Good company also consists of those who love each other for the sake of Allah without a hidden agenda. We learned from the narration of Abu Hurayrah, may Allah be pleased with him, in Riyad Al-Saliheen, that some of the people who will be under the shade of the throne of Allah on the day where there is no shade except His shade are "two men who meet and love each other and depart from each other for the sake of Allah." These are the good companions, and the best company to keep.

The companions we keep have an effect on our mindsets. Good companions help motivate us, keep us away from sins, and help us feel closer to Allah. Abu Musa Al-Ashari, may Allah be pleased with him said, "I heard the Prophet, peace be upon him, saying, "The example of good company and bad company is that of the owner of musk (perfume salesman) and of the one blowing the bellows (blacksmith). The owner of musk offers you some free of charge, or you would buy it from him, or you smell its pleasant fragrance; and as for the one who blows the bellows (blacksmith), he either burns your clothes or you smell its repugnant smell."[11]

This hadith shows that we are positively or negatively affected by the companions we keep. I will discuss the first part of the hadith in regards to the seller of perfume in this portion. The good companions are like musk--pure and pleasant. He is one of the most valuable assets in one's life, and a cause for enrichment of one's happiness and good deeds. A good companion has a beautiful character and manners, which will rub off on you if you continue being around him or her just like the

---

[11] Al-Nawawi, Imam Muhyu Al-Din Abu Zakariya Ibn Yahya Ibn Sharaf. *Riyad Al-Saliheen. (Lahor:* Maktaba-e-Rehmania). Print.

perfume's scent that seeps into your clothing, and makes them smell pleasant. A good companion brings a smile to your face, treats you kindly, and wishes for you what he wishes for himself. Therefore, no harm will come to you from him, and when he offers you advice, he does so sincerely. He has no ulterior motives. He protects you in your absence, and is one whom you could trust with your possessions, wealth, or even your life. He calls you to Allah, and so you will remain successful in both worlds, because he looks out for you in terms of your worldly life and the hereafter and has your best interest at heart.

You must have witnessed the benefits of the good companion in your own life when, for example, you saw them doing a good deed, and it encouraged you to start doing the same good deed as well. Maybe they were very generous and kind, and so you also began to give more charity and became more generous. Or maybe you are friends with someone who is very timely in their prayers, and it creates a desire in you to perform your prayers on time as well. They are the good company to keep.

Allah often tells us in the Quran to keep good company, and to be in the company of those who pray, those who are truthful, and those who have patience. Allah states, "Oh, those who believe, persevere in patience and constancy, and vie each other in patience, and strengthen each other, and fear Allah, perhaps that you might prosper," (3:200). Allah also states in the Quran, "Oh those who believe, fear Allah and be among those who are truthful," (9:119). Allah, the Exalted, even advised Maryam, peace be upon her, to keep good company as well by saying, "Oh Maryam, be obedient to your Lord, and prostrate and bow down with those who bow down," (3:43), and Allah also said to Prophet Mohammad, peace be upon him, "So glorify your Lord with praise, and be with those who prostrate," (Quran, 15:98). We learn from these verses that the best of creations were advised to be in the company of good people, and we are in more need of such companions. If we follow the advice of Allah, we will find prosperity in the company of good people inshallah.

Perhaps one of the best verses to illustrate the necessity of good companions is when Allah says in the Quran, chapter 18:28, "And keep yourself attached to those who call upon their Lord, morning and evening, seeking His pleasure, and do not turn your eyes away from them, seeking the adornments of the life of this world, and obey not the one whose heart We have rendered heedless of Our remembrance, one who follows his desires, and one whose fate is in total loss." This verse is perfect in that it shows who the good companion is as well as whom we should avoid and stay away from, which are the people who are unaware and heedless of Allah, and those whose only aim is worldly pleasures.

I will also mention that being surrounded with good companions is better than being in solitude. When we are alone, we are easy prey for Shaitan, but when we are together, and united upon the good, we become stronger and our resolve and conviction becomes unwavering. Good company has the capacity to help us remain steadfast upon the religion of Allah, strengthen our hearts, and help us become more hopeful, positive, and optimistic. Therefore, being around such people will helps us develop the Muslim mindset with more ease and fluidity.

We have established that the company you keep has an effect on your mindset, perspective, and worldview, thereby your actions. One of the quickest ways to ruin your day or your life is to be around people who exude negativity. They cannot help it. It might even have become a part of their nature. These are the bad companions, and the company you don't want to be around. These are the blacksmiths you should avoid. Let's look at who the bad companion is in regards to what the Prophet, peace be upon him, mentioned when he compared the blacksmith to the bad companion.

A bad companion like the blacksmith causes you pain and damage, which can sometimes be irreversible just like your clothing being burnt. You will reek of black smoke and find black dust on your clothing and skin. It is unbearable being near a furnace where the blacksmith works just as it is unbearable being with a bad companion who might be hot-tempered and detrimental to your being. Bad companions invite people to do evil, bad manners, speak negatively, and even think negatively. Bad companions will taint and ruin your character similar to your clothing being burnt, which will have holes in it due to the sparks that are a byproduct of this type of work. They will take advantage of you for their own benefit, and care little about your wellbeing. They don't offer you sincere advice and in fact, they would be jealous of you if you were to be successful. Thus, they prevent you from progressing in life, calling you towards that which Allah has forbidden and leave you in the lurch in your time of need.

Bad companions also encourage you to commit sins, and influence you negatively by infecting you with their pessimism, and drowning you in their repugnant smell of their bad character, mannerisms, and negative view of the world. Being around bad companions has catastrophic consequences, and we may not recognize it until we are plunged into heedlessness and negativity ourselves. Being in such a state will have terrible effects on your relationships with your spouse, children, parents, siblings, relatives, friends, and your community. It will even affect your relationships and interactions with strangers. The most fatal effect of negative companionship is on our akhira, because the outcome of that might be eternal. For these reasons, it is vital that we surround ourselves with the most sincere, benevolent, and supportive group of people who want us to succeed not just in our worldly lives, but rather more importantly, in the hereafter. Progress, success and prosperity has been linked to being in good company, and so we must choose wisely whom we want in our lives.

Surround Yourself with People of Accountability

There needs to be someone in your life who holds you accountable to a higher standard of character, mannerisms, and your relationship with Allah and His creation. This needs to be someone who is not afraid to be direct with you and who will not sugarcoat anything. It should be someone who wants what is best for you and someone whom you can trust to keep what you talk about in confidence. It can be your parents, teachers, older siblings, a long-term friend, or even a community member. My teachers regularly ask the other students and I if we read the Quran, did tahajjud (night prayer), fasted, and memorized certain duas (supplications or prophetic prayers) and parts of the Quran.

By asking us, it is a constant reminder for us to be better people. It causes happiness in my heart that there is someone who cares and is concerned for our akhira (our life after death). Although our intentions are for Allah, the reminders force us not to disappoint our teachers and to be even better than what they are asking of us.

Alhamdulillah, (all praise be to Allah), I am blessed to have parents and teachers who care so much. Inshallah, you, too, can benefit immensely by surrounding yourself with people who hold you to a higher standard and people who encourage you to be better than yesterday.

Having someone to guide you along and even hold your hand on a daily basis amplifies your success in achieving a Muslim mindset, because you will see the progress you are making. As you progress in your goals and achievements, it will propel you in striving even more in every endeavor, and slowly relieve you of any negativity you may have towards yourself. It will also slowly erode away any self-limiting beliefs you may have about your abilities and capacity to be an accomplished person.

Inshallah make dua to Allah to surround you with people who hold you to a higher standard, and who cause you to strive daily to reach for your fullest potential.

Remove Yourself From the Company of Toxic People

There may be one or multiple people in your life who somehow find a way to make you feel bad, belittle you, gossip, or spread rumors and stories about you. Whether it is out of jealousy or hatred, or any other reason, only Allah knows, but you need to steer clear of such people. Sometimes, no matter what you do or how much you try to be kind and forgiving to them, somehow they still find a way to hurt you.

If this is the case with you, forgive them and move on with your life. You might ask, "How can I? They are my relatives." I am not asking you to break relations here, I am only saying don't allow yourself to be a victim of the same circumstances over and over again. You should still be respectful and say salam, but it doesn't mean that you have to be best friends. You don't have to share your deep secrets with them or involve them in your life. Otherwise, they may poke you and push you to such an extent that you will react in a way that is very damaging to you and others.

Save yourself, your honor, and your reputation by avoiding these people. There is a reason why they are called "toxic." They poison every part of your life and hurt you to such an extent that you can barely lift your eyes. Being around such people might become a cause for becoming a person with a negative mindset, feeling bad about yourself and feeling angry and/or even depressed. So, gracefully avoid toxic people and surround yourself with the good companions we discussed earlier.

Avoid Company That Leads to Arguments and Anger

Refrain from having arguments with anyone, and refrain from people who are argumentative. Arguments are one of the quickest ways to ruin your good day, and it can lead to anger. Feelings of anger and frustration have physical effects on your body. It puts you in the fight-or-flight mode, where your heart rate increases, your breathing becomes faster, and your muscles contract and become tense, which cannot be sustained for long periods of time. This is a sign that you need to back away and avoid the situation.

When you become angry, you literally lose the ability to think straight, and you will end up doing and sayings things that you would never have done in a calm and relaxed environment. Therefore, if you even sense a negative situation about to take place, even as mild as something being exchanged by barely looking at the other person, remove yourself from the situation. You have too many important goals to accomplish, and too much at stake, so don't allow yourself to get trapped in other people's negativity.

Having said that, don't hold grudges against anyone. Every night when you go to sleep, forgive everyone, including yourself. When you forgive someone who has hurt you so deeply and really made you question your entire existence, it feels like a mountain has been lifted off of you. Thus it becomes easier to develop a positive mindset as a Muslim.

The company we keep influences our mindsets. Therefore, it is vital that we surround ourselves with people who are the good companions, and avoid befriending bad companions. We also need to surround ourselves with people who will hold us accountable, and avoid those who are argumentative and toxic. As we surround ourselves with positive, optimistic, and good people, our view of the world also becomes positive, optimistic and we become more apt to developing the Muslim mindset.

Lesson 4:
Practice Forgiveness Daily

THE act of forgiveness is incredibly important in achieving a Muslim mindset. Forgiveness makes up a major part of the Muslim's life, because at one point or another, many of us face heartaches, pain and utter negativity. It is for this reason we explore the necessity of forgiveness in developing a Muslim mindset in this lesson, and the steps we can take to become more forgiving.

We all need forgiveness. Sometimes we need our own forgiveness more than anyone else's forgiveness, because so often, we are too hard on ourselves, and we would never treat anyone else like that. We criticize and even ridicule ourselves for the mistakes we have made, for the actions we took, and the actions we didn't take. We bombard ourselves with thoughts of negativity, belittling and reducing our own self-worth to nothingness.

Maybe we said something we shouldn't have said, did something we shouldn't have done, or we are not in life where we would like to be. You see other people moving ahead, and you look down upon yourself for not having the same go-getter spirit and attitude, or you fault yourself for having tried different things and ideas, but none of them have worked.

Maybe you have made decisions you are not proud of. You may have reached a plateau, and you don't know what to do. You are confused and lost, and uncertainty envelopes you from every corner. You have constant thoughts of "I should have done this," or "If only I had done that," or you are dreading, "What if this happens?" or "What if that happens?"

I just want you to know that, for many people, these thoughts are all too common. It doesn't make you a bad person; rather, it shows how human you are. You are in need of some direction, but not an intervention, because what you are feeling is normal.

Usually, it is our own selves who wear us down. Most people usually leave us alone, and in fact, treat us very kindly and beautifully. We are the ones who usually initiate these thoughts and perpetuate their existence. Of course, you have to keep in mind that Shaitan is always whispering to you, and he has nothing good to say. The good news is that there is a solution to all of your self-criticism and negative self-talk.

Forgiveness.

Forgiveness is the solution to it all.

When you understand the power of forgiveness, life will become so much easier for you to live. I will explain the reasoning of why forgiveness is so important to learn and even hopefully master inshallah.

The Psychology of Forgiveness: Why We Should Let Go

Why should we forgive?

The reasons are far too many. Harboring anger and resentments towards ourselves and/or others is emotionally, physically, mentally, and spiritually unhealthy. It negatively impacts your relationships, hinders your progress, and prevents you from growing as a person and truly blossoming into the person you are meant to be.

Those who are unable to forgive suffer from depression, are unhappy, and treat others unkindly, all of which further perpetuates their negativity. It is self-destructive. Therefore, it hinders the development of the Muslim mindset.

Some medical practices have started a new therapeutic approach of forgiveness therapy (FT) to help patients heal faster. Forgiveness leads to a faster recovery in burn patients or people who have surgeries. We have been taught in nursing that patients who are emotionally healthy are able to heal faster, and their stay in the hospital is shorter, which can be achieved by practicing forgiveness. We learned that patients' recovery is greatly impacted by their ability to forgive, let go, and find peace. This shows that their emotional and spiritual wellbeing has a direct effect on their recovery. Their mindset helps determine the outcomes of their health. Usually, a person who enjoys great emotional and spiritual health has learned how to forgive his own self and others. Moreover, forgiveness reduces stress levels, anxiety, depression, and ensures a better quality of life, all of which are necessary in the development and achievement of the Muslim mindset.

We see the amazing results of forgiveness in this new form of therapy. Through forgiveness therapy, developmental psychologist Robert Enright, in his study, learned that his patients, who were suffering from heart disease, had better blood flow to the heart, and he saw tremendous success in the reduction of substance abuse for those dealing with addiction. The subjects who attended forgiveness therapy reported feeling less depressed and anxious, there was an improvement in their self-image, and they were less vulnerable to drug abuse than the control group.

Alhumdulillah, all of this is just supplemental proof of what Allah has stated so many times in the Quran about forgiveness being better for us. Allah states in chapter 42, verse 40, that whoever forgives, and makes reconciliation, his reward is with Allah. He also states that whoever shows patience and forgives, that would be truly from the things recommended by Allah (40:43). These are but two paraphrased verses, and the Quran is filled with verses of forgiveness mashallah. Often, Allah refers to Himself as The Most Forgiving and The Most Merciful. The quality of forgiveness is a noble, and an upright characteristic that all of us should strive day and night to attain inshallah.

Below I share with you the steps on how to forgive and let go in order to design a life that is meaningful to you, a life that brings you peace and illuminates both of your worlds inshallah.

Forgive Yourself

Although this process can be gut wrenching, it will have compounding positive effects inshallah. Forgiving yourself will require you to be absolutely honest with yourself. It will hurt, and it might even make you cry. It is an emotional and painful process, because it requires you to take responsibility for your actions, and it brings to the forefront what you may have been trying to hide for a long time. It will showcase to you your weaknesses, faults, and mistakes. As human beings, we are usually not too fond of admitting even to our own selves such things. As difficult a process as forgiving ourselves is, it is also incredibly rewarding and freeing alhumdulillah.

Therefore, begin by coming to terms with yourself, and then forgive all of your faults, mistakes, and weaknesses. You can do that by sitting in a quiet place, after your salah or in front of the mirror by looking straight into your eyes, so that you know that there is no running from this. Begin by stating what you need to forgive yourself for.

For example

"I forgive you for not taking the time to take care of yourself, while you were busy taking care of others."

"I forgive you for the choices you have made that have impacted you negatively." [Be specific.]

"I forgive you for being so hard on yourself."

Forgive yourself for whatever it is that you need forgiveness for, and it is best to mention your name at the beginning of your forgiveness statement. Be completely honest with yourself. No one has to know what you forgive yourself for.

Every day, think of at least three to five things you need forgiveness for. Stay consistent, even if you have to forgive yourself for the same thing every single day. Continue this practice until the weight of what you need to forgive yourself for finally dissipates and you are free of it inshallah. Fill up the newfound space that you now have in your thoughts that was originally taken up by your negativity towards yourself with kindness and love towards yourself. Fill it with positive thoughts about yourself, and focus on your good qualities.

Ask for Forgiveness

First, ask for forgiveness from Allah, and be regretful about what it is that you have done. This is also a recognition of our weak human nature and our perfection in imperfection. We are built by nature to do things we are not supposed to do, because we have free will. This, however, does not mean that we should continue the same mistakes, faults, and sins indefinitely. We have been given the capabilities to be upright, so there are no excuses.

When we recognize our shortcomings, we should immediately ask for forgiveness from Allah. Resolve not to repeat the same sins or faults again. And if you do, then ask for forgiveness again, and make a firm intention not to go back to your sins. Continue this process until you feel completely free of it inshallah.

Asking for forgiveness from Allah is easier than asking people to forgive you. The process alone of asking for forgiveness, be it from one's self, Allah, or other people, requires us to humble ourselves. However, it is most difficult when you ask others for forgiveness. Apologizing and saying you're sorry to others can be hard, because we feel guilty, and we don't know what the other person's reaction will be. If it has to be done, do it inshallah in a beautiful and calm demeanor.

This also means that you should forgive others quickly. Don't harbor hurt feelings inside your heart. Let it go immediately, otherwise you will be carrying around unwanted burdens for the remainder of your life. When nothing is weighing you down, it is easier to focus, strive, and be successful in whatever your endeavors may be inshallah. So, just let it go.

Be one of those people who quickly forgive others so that inshallah the same blessings can be extended towards you. In chapter 24 of the Quran, verse 22, Allah sates, "let not those among you who are endued with sufficient means resolve by oath against helping their kinsmen, those who are in need, and those who have emigrated in Allah's cause: Let them forgive and overlook, do you not wish that Allah should forgive you? For indeed, Allah is Most Forgiving and Most Merciful."

This verse is referring to the most beloved companion Abu Bakr, may Allah be pleased with him. His maternal cousin was one of the people who had spread slander against his daughter, Aisha, may Allah be pleased with her. Aisha was the wife of Prophet Mohammad, peace be upon him. Allah exonerated her of the charges of adultery that had been casted against her, and showed what a pious and upright woman she was. Abu Bakr, may Allah be pleased with him, cried for his daughter, and understood the serious ramifications of such false charges against pious women, let alone the wife of the most beloved man to Allah in the entire existence of the universe.

As stated in Ibn Kathir, naturally, Abu Bakr, may Allah be pleased with him, was hurt and took an oath that he would no longer financially support his cousin. However, Allah revealed to him that forgiveness is better, and wouldn't he like that Allah forgives him too? So Abu Bakr, may Allah be pleased with him, said, "Yes, I love that You should forgive us, our Lord!" Then he continued to financially support his poor cousin and said, "by

Allah, I will never deprive him of it," even though before that he had said, "Never will I give him anything of benefit."

What is fascinating about this verse is even though the accusation against Aisha, may Allah be pleased with her, was so enormous, once she was exonerated and the ones who slandered her were punished, Allah wanted forgiveness amongst each other, and did not want grudges to exist between anyone. We are ordered to forgive again and again, and to overlook all negative treatment, because we are all brothers and sisters in reality and Allah's forgiveness is better for us.

When we forgive others, let's not mistake it for doing that person a favor. We are doing it for Allah and ourselves, because we wouldn't want our entrance to Jannah to be delayed on the Day of Judgment just because we have to settle a dispute that could have been easily forgiven in this life.

Let's not be one of those people who carry around our baggage from one world to the next. We want to enter Jannah as soon as possible inshallah. We want Allah to forgive us, and so we should forgive others. Inshallah you will see the benefits of forgiveness in your life in both worlds.

How magnificent is our Allah that He said forgiveness is better for us. We are doing ourselves a favor by forgiving others. Some people might not fully understand this if they have not had to forgive others, but such cases are rare. When you actually forgive others, it frees you from the shackles that had chained you to your anger, frustration, and burdens. You will be able to focus on your own life, move on and develop the Muslim mindset.

Forgiveness allows you to heal and to heal others who may be suffering as well. It grants you the ability to understand others and what is truly important and meaningful in life. This newfound understanding is incredible in achieving a mindset that is rooted in the Islamic ideals of hope, optimism, and always expecting the best from Allah.

Say NO to "What if ..."

Many of us often find ourselves constantly belittling ourselves and having frustrating thoughts, because somehow, we think that we could have changed the outcome if we had done something differently in the past.

The truth is that this kind of mindset is an influence of Shaitan. So, whenever you find yourself in this kind of ruckus, stop yourself immediately. Abu Hurayrah, may Allah be pleased with him, narrated that the Prophet peace be upon him, said, "A strong believer is better and dearer to Allah than a weak one, and both are good. Adhere to that which is beneficial for you. Keep asking Allah for help, and do not refrain from it. If you are afflicted in any way, do not say: 'If I had done this or that, it would have been like such and such,' but only say: 'Allah determined it so, and did as He willed.'"

This hadith should be a relief for every Muslim, and we should be grateful to Allah for removing from us the burden of responsibility we feel for those things, which are not in our control. We should accept our current circumstances, and become grateful for whatever it is that Allah has granted to us.

Accept that You Don't Have All the Answers

You don't know the unseen, you don't know what will happen tomorrow, and you don't know what would have happened in the past if you had changed something. Resolve to be excited for what life has to offer, whatever it may be inshallah, because it is all from Allah. This also means that whatever negativity you may harbor as a result towards yourself needs to be forgiven by you so that you can continue on your journey to achieving a Muslim mindset.

It may cause you a bit of anxiety, because you don't know what the future holds for you, but that is the exact same reason you should look forward to whatever is to come. Of course, we only have good hopes and wish for the best from Allah.

Our imaginations are too limited, which is why we can't possibly know what Allah has to offer us in our worldly future, or even in the hereafter. What is true, and I have experienced this in my own life, is that reality is far better than any and every imagination. This world is so beautiful, and yet we spend quite a lot of our time lost in our thoughts and imaginations, instead of choosing to live the life we have already been blessed with. So, enjoy your current state of affairs and be hopeful about your future inshallah.

Accept Qadr

What hit would have never missed and what missed would have never hit. What this means is that whatever Allah had destined to happen, it could in no way have been averted or happened differently. It also means that whatever was not decreed by Allah, the Exalted, could in no way come to fruition. It is qadr or predestination. Therefore, whatever it is that took place in your life, it already happened, and you cannot change it.

What you can change, however, is what you do about it, how you perceive and feel about it, and what you choose to learn from it. Knowing that there is only so much that you can control, and the rest is in the hands of Allah, absolves you of responsibility and accountability, which should be a sense of relief for everyone. You don't have to worry about the outcome, because Allah will take care of that for you. Just do your part and leave the rest to Allah.

Also, remember that the pens have lifted and the pages have dried, because Allah already wrote everything down since the beginning of time. Therefore, there is no need to worry about the future nor can you change any of your past. Accept life as it is, and change only that which is in your power inshallah. It is one of our core beliefs to accept all of the situations, past or present, in our lives that we cannot do anything about. So, endure patiently, live meaningfully, and remember that Allah is ever aware of your situation.

Whatever comes to you, know that Allah's wisdom encompasses all things. Inshallah you may not realize it now, but there will come a time when you will appreciate your mistakes, delays, and hardships, and you will realize their purpose in your life. Be patient and kind to yourself inshallah, because what is yours will be yours anyway.

So, let go and forgive yourself and others. Every night before you go to sleep, forgive everyone. If it is not in your habit to forgive, don't worry inshallah. Ask Allah to soften your heart and to make you one of those people who has mercy for others. Whoever shows mercy to others, Allah will show him mercy as well inshallah.

When you consistently implement any of the steps talked about in this section about forgiveness, you will find it natural to have a positive Muslim mindset inshallah. When your relationships with your parents, family, teachers, friends and anyone else you deem important in your life are positive and at peace, it will positively affect other aspects of your life as well. You will slowly find it easier to have a meaningful life inshallah that is based on the Muslim mindset.

Take one point from any of the above, and work on practicing it whether it is forgiveness towards yourself or others. As you accomplish one of them, then move on to the next so that you can become whole again. Allah will make it easy for you to achieve a positive Muslim mindset and live life the way you were meant to live. May Allah make us from amongst those people who forgive and are forgiven easily. Ameen.

Lesson 5:
Keep Your Health Intact

IT really is true that you don't know what you have until you lose it. Health is one of those things. When you are healthy and in great condition, you forget what an astronomical blessing it is. We take our good health for granted and don't realize that if we lose it, it becomes difficult to live our lives meaningfully, worship Allah and even more difficult to maintain a positive mindset, a Muslim mindset.

When you are not feeling your best, and are bogged down by negative thoughts, begin by looking good. You have probably heard that the first step to feeling good is looking good. It is more important than some people realize.

Work on yourself and your health. Maintain a healthy weight. Notice, I said a *healthy* weight, meaning that one should not strive for an unrealistic weight and look unhealthy. Be kind to yourself and don't over exert yourself. The most lasting and permanent changes are those that are acquired consistently and persistently over a long period of time.

Time will pass by anyway, so there is no reason to hurry and be hasty. Take small and consistent steps in maintaining a healthy weight and preventing diseases. The most important factor is that you should strive to preserve your ability to worship Allah in the most excellent state.

Eat Right

You can outwardly look good and inwardly feel whole by learning to eat well, and ultimately feel great about yourself. You really are what you eat. Whatever you eat is taken up by your cells and used to make new cells, and eventually, it even changes your DNA. Having this knowledge should make us excited and strive towards good diet practices so that we can achieve long-lasting and healthy results. This is also why it is so important to stay away from haram meats and haram products, because we do not want the makeup of our being to consist of haram. In the Quran, we learn that when The Companions of the Cave woke up after about three hundred and nine years, one of the first things they were concerned with was eating the "purest" and healthiest food.[12] We should strive for eating the most purest and best of foods so that we can satisfy our hunger and embody the best examples in our religion.

In nursing, we learned that your health is 80% what you eat and 20% exercise. For many of us, this is probably one of the best things we have ever learned, because it means that we only have to control our consumption of food. At the same time, many of us become extremely saddened by this, because we feel that it is difficult to control how we eat because of the unhealthy habits we have formed over many years.

I think it is good news. It highlights what many of us already know to be true: we have control over our health and wellbeing. Knowing this fact allows us to make better choices about our diets. Healthy diets consist mainly of eating more green and colorful vegetables, fruits, and whole grains. There is valuable information available to us online, and in books to help us make smart decisions regarding our health.

That being said, however, there is no need to eat three meals a day with a snack in between each. This means that during your waking hours, were you to follow such an eating schedule, you would be eating almost every two to three hours.

---

[12] 18:19

Your body does not need so much food. When your meals are so close together, it keeps your body in constant sugar fluctuations, which is devastating to your body, mind, and soul. It is certainly not the sunnah, which is the way and example of the Prophet Mohammad, peace be upon him.

Our bodies need rest, and they need to remove the free radicals, toxins, and inflammatory agents that move around or stay stagnant, destroying us from the inside out. Our cells need time to repair, and heal. If our bodies don't rest, and we allow them to be in constant sugar fluctuations, it leads to heart disease, strokes, and obesity.

Eating too much also causes fatigue, restlessness, or over-sleeping, and it depletes you of your energy. If your digestive system is unnecessarily busy digesting food, the brain redirects the blood there, instead of to the brain. This is why you feel so tired after having a meal, especially a large, greasy, unhealthy meal. The body expends too much energy in digestion. This is why fasting is so important, and why constantly eating is so detrimental to our health. You really don't need to eat more than twice a day, unless you have a very fast metabolism, or you are expending more energy, which is usually the case with athletes.

Many of us have also adopted fatigue as a lifestyle, and we accept it as normal. We are stressed out, frustrated, and we have adopted really poor diet habits. We literally eat non-food: food that has been cooked up or processed in some factory that has all sorts of non-food items in it and has actually managed to make it through the Food and Drug Administration regulations and then it is sold to us. It is more vital than ever to make a habit of eating nutritious and healthy foods in order to feel energized and maintain the ability to live meaningfully.

Exercise Regularly

Eating well is the main and most important path to taking care of our physical health. However, we can also raise our energy levels and feel great about ourselves by exercising. You can do this by exercising three to five times per week for thirty minutes at least. If this is too hard to do in the beginning, because it has not yet become a habit, do what is most easy for you. You can even begin by doing it once a week for fifteen minutes.

Exercising once a week for several weeks or even months for fifteen minutes is better than not doing it at all. We should strive towards forming good habits, even if they are small. Once we have mastered small doable habits, we can then aim for higher, and more challenging ones inshallah.

If you are one of those people who just can't seem to get going no matter what you do, and you have literally tried everything, then start with exercises that don't intimidate you at all. In the beginning, just start by stretching. Stretching is easy, and you really don't need anything outside of yourself to get going. There is no need for dumbbells, or exercise machines, and treadmills. Just stretch.

Continue to do that for a few weeks until it has become easy for you and you have made a habit out of it. Slowly add doable exercises that are easy for you, but still cause your heart to beat faster. As you begin to start your workouts, you can increase either the amount of time or the intensity of the exercise. You can even add another exercise to it like going from stretching alone to adding abdominal exercises. All you need is your body and a big enough space where your safety is not compromised. Don't be so hard on yourself and expect unrealistic results that make you leave the workouts altogether. The important thing to take away here is to cultivate good health habits that make you feel energetic, and make you feel good about your outer and inner self.

When you are exercising, focus on your spine and your joints. The spine is the mainframe and foundation of the body. If the spine is in great condition, the rest of the body, including your muscles, will follow suit. When you are exercising, integrate exercises that will strengthen your spine. This is why stretching and yoga are perfect for back pain or just having a strong core.

In the beginning, you will have to be patient. So no matter how much you look in the mirror, you are not going to see any sudden magical changes. Be patient with yourself and continue exercising.

Make it your habit to stay hydrated, take care of your skin, and dress neatly and beautifully. Our Prophet, peace be always upon him, mentioned in a close translation, "Verily, Allah is beautiful and He loves beauty."[13] Therefore, don't feel bad if you like to look nice. Everyone should have that desire, and it is not a sign of arrogance. Arrogance is when you deem other people lower than yourself. May Allah protect us from such thoughts and beliefs. Ameen. However, don't expend so much energy and money trying to look good that it is the only thing you focus on. Be balanced in how you spend your time and health. Inshallah as you feel better about yourself, it will have a positive impact on your mindset and help you feel great.

---

[13] Al-Bulandshehri, 53

Manage Stress

I have been increasingly noticing that many Muslims are stressed, and feel unsatisfied with their lives. With increasing demands on our time and energy at work, school, family, and our own personal lives, stress has become a normal coping mechanism for many people. However, it doesn't have to be. There are healthier ways of coping with stressful situations, eliminating anxiety and even feeling overwhelmed. We can learn to cope, adapt, and find peace, and meaning in our lives while having a demanding work or family life.

Some stress can actually be good for you. It is called eustress. Good stress can help you become stronger, perform better, and get tasks done faster. It can be motivating and exciting at the same time. This is provided that eustress comes in small doses, so that you don't feel overwhelmed. For example, an approaching deadline can motivate you to get your work done, and complete it with excellence, because you will be hyper-focused, and the amount of energy you spend on this project will be balanced. You can relax afterwards, and enjoy your free time doing activities that make you feel relaxed and at peace. In this type of situation, we usually feel accomplished and feel good about ourselves.

However, if you have a series of deadlines, a public speech to give that you are not prepared for, family obligations, and are in debt, then this is called negative stress. Having multiple constraints can hinder your progress, overwhelm you and cause you to feel like your drowning in too many obligations. It does not allow you time for yourself so that you can recover and maintain balance.

Negative stress can trigger the fight-or-flight response, which is the body's way of protecting you from danger. The first situation in which you only had one deadline, you were motivated to get your work done and finish it on time. This means that you were in the fight mode, and ready to face the project head on. In the latter example, you are overwhelmed by too many obligations. There can be one of two outcomes in this scenario: some people will flee from the situation altogether, while others become paralyzed, and don't do anything. They become stopped in their tracks, unable to move, and just sit or stand there.

If you ever see a wild or carnivorous animal, let's say a lion, chances are most of you are not going to fight it, so that we might establish who is the biggest King of the jungle. Most of you will either be running for your lives or freeze and feel paralyzed. This is the flight response, or better yet, the fright response. You will feel numb, and unable to move, at which point, you might become food. May Allah save you.

This is the kind of situation we want to avoid. We want to avoid feeling helpless and as though we are not in control. Feeling a lack of control over our lives is stressful. It hinders productivity, and it diminishes our capacity to achieve our goals. It is a negative cycle that continues to feed our pessimistic mindsets.

As human beings, we cannot endure long periods in a heightened state of fight-or-flight response where our heart rate and breathing is increased, our muscles are contracted, and our pupils are dilated. It cannot be sustained for long, and we cannot thrive in such stressful environments. This is why people get stress-ulcers, heart attacks, strokes, and even multiple sclerosis. These are fatal, painful and difficult processes to go through. The thing is that this can be avoided by employing certain actions to decrease our stress levels and maintain relative control.

The question this puts forth then is, "How can we live in a way in which we can control our lives, and protect ourselves from feeling stressed and overwhelmed?"

There are many solutions that can help alleviate stress so that you are always feeling at your best, even on your worst days. Some things you might find helpful in lessening stress is talking to someone trustworthy and asking for their guidance or just sharing how you have been feeling with them. In the moment, however, the first thing you need to do is to just breathe, and take a step back from everything. Whenever you are feeling like it is just too much, sit quietly or lie down and breathe. Focus on the rise and fall of your chest so that your thoughts calm down and become synchronized with the pattern of your breathing. Deep breaths give you the ability to take your life into perspective, and zoom out from your current situation. It allows you to observe your life from an outsider's perspective and find solutions that you previously couldn't even think about, because you were so stressed and overwhelmed. Make a habit of deep breathing, and allow yourself to zoom out of your life for a few minutes every day, after salah or at least once a week. Deliberately find time for this practice.

Lessen your load. Think about your priorities. What must get done? Usually, the main priorities are one or two things. Do them first. Is there anything that someone else can do? If a certain task can be delegated to someone else, and it is not required that you do it, then delegate it. Then, think about what can be eliminated completely. If you don't have to do it, and there are no penalties for it, then don't allow it to contribute to your heightened state. Eliminate it. It is okay and recommended to ask for help, especially from people who already love you and want to show their love and affection for you.

So remember to prioritize, delegate, and eliminate. Lessening the amount of tasks and/or chores we feel we need to do is incredibly relieving and contributes tremendously to feeling balanced.

Sometimes, just go with the flow. You don't have to control everything. Just let things be. If it is not immediately necessary to change it or attend to it, then let it be. Don't take on more than you can handle. You want to be able to get up the next morning and not feel anxious and overwhelmed by the day ahead.

Getting tasks done and taking action is an important part of de-stressing. However, don't be so task-oriented that you forget to enjoy life altogether. Find something that works for you. Carve out time for yourself daily or weekly that is just for you alone, and no one else. Do an activity that makes you happy, and brings out your creative side. It should be relaxing and help you feel at ease. It should lead to feeling optimistic and appreciative of your health and the life you have been gifted by Allah.

The way you cope with stress does not need to resemble other people's ways. Be open to many permissible possibilities, and let Allah be your guide. You can read a good book, exercise, go out in nature, and call up your friends and spend time together. Refrain from reverting back to negative thinking or any thoughts that cause you stress.

You can always turn to Allah, and pray to Him. Ask Allah for ease, and a better way to help you overcome stress, stay healthy, and maintain a positive mindset inshallah. Continue gracefully on your journey of eating right, exercising, and managing stress. Slowly, you will see amazing results in your health and wellbeing, and ultimately enjoy the benefits of the Muslim mindset.

Lesson 6:
Think Positive

FOR many, thinking positive is likely one of the most difficult challenges they may have ever contended with. I personally don't like to think of anything as difficult, because once it is registered in my brain as "difficult," then naturally, I stay away from it. I tend not to tell others that something is difficult either, and it is rare that anything is so difficult that it cannot be accomplished.

Alhamdulillah, most challenges in this life can be overcome and almost anything is doable. Understanding this concept is important, because it has a direct effect on our mindsets. When we believe that the goals we have for ourselves are doable, the burden and frustration we might feel otherwise is lifted off of us.

Truly, anything that a man or woman has the ability to do, can be done. This also means that if other people can do it, so can you. This is why having a Muslim mindset is important, which begins with your thoughts. Below, I will outline a list of ways you can improve your thoughts and help shift them from pessimistic to optimistic patterns.

One of the first actions you can take early in the morning is to start the day strong. You can do this by having an easy-to-follow routine that works for you. Get all of your most important tasks done early in the day, being really keen on completing them with excellence, but not necessarily perfection. Don't be one of those people who want to complete every task to perfection and end up not doing anything at all. Just start your routine inshallah, and with a consistent effort, you can begin to complete them with excellence.

If you don't have a routine, begin by thinking about what is most important and urgent that needs to get done right away. Try to avoid having too many tasks that are *urgent*, because they cause undue stress to your health and wellbeing. It is much better to have important tasks to do that don't have a daunting deadline attached to them that make you feel overwhelmed and stressed. Just relax and keep a moderate pace in completing your work. Life is easy, alhamdulillah, so don't make it difficult for yourself.

Don't Dwell on Negative Thoughts

Dwelling on negative thoughts is counter-productive to having a positive mindset. Focusing on negativity hinders us from acquiring a mindset that is rooted in improving our thoughts, so that it can translate into positive results over time.

Therefore, it is vital to do away with all thoughts of negativity, dwelling on the past or mistakes we have made and probably will continue to make. Make it a habit to catch yourself as soon as you begin to think something negative. Practice allowing yourself to let the thoughts flow, looking for the negative patterns that exist in your thought processes, which is so common for many of us. When you notice the negative thoughts or patterns of negativity, nip them in the bud. Put a stop to them right away.

This will require consistent effort over time, because for years, we have hard-wired these bad habits of negative thinking patterns into our brains. We don't even think about how negative our thoughts can be, because they have become a habit and a comfortable zone for us to be in. It is kind of like driving home from school or work, and you don't know how you got there. You have driven the same route so many times that without even thinking about it, your brain has learned how to get you home mashallah. The brain is amazing.

The good news is that negative thought patterns can be replaced with better and more positive and healing thoughts.

If you are faced with a difficult situation, remind yourself to stay positive, and that Allah wants ease for you. He does not want difficulty for you, and He is only a prostration away from you. Inshallah there is always hope in every difficulty. Always look for the positive in any and every situation.

Think Highly of Yourself

I don't mean this in an arrogant manner; rather, we have to accept and understand who we are as people, and recognize our excellence that has been bestowed upon us by Allah. Allah has created the human being in the best shape and form with the best of features.[14] Allah has given the human being intelligence and abilities not shared by any other creature. We are *ashraful makhluqat*, the noblest, highest, and best of the creations.

To illustrate this point further, Allah said in the Quran, in chapter 17:70, "And indeed, We have honored the children of Adam, and carried them upon the land and sea and provided for them of

---

[14] Quran 82:7, 94:5

the good things and preferred them over much of the creation, with a marked preference." Ibn Kathir, may Allah be pleased with him, says that the human being has been given such blessings as has never been given to any other creation of Allah before us: we have the best form, stature, walk on two instead of four, and Allah gave us the faculties of hearing, seeing, feeling, and thinking, with which we know what is good and what is evil, and have been provided all sources of life as sustenance. What is most amazing about the above verse is that Ibn Kathir quoted this Holy verse "as a proof for the superiority of mankind over angels." So you see, by default, you are an incredible being. You are more beloved to Allah than the angels, no matter how broken, sinful, or a bad person you might think you are.

I do recognize that as difficulties, mistakes, and bad experiences occur in our lives, we tend to focus on the negative instead of also appreciating the good in us. As a result, our self-esteem usually suffers. It is often due to us blaming and being hard on ourselves, and generally, we would not treat others in the same manner. We wouldn't be so harsh on our loved ones nor would we blame them to such an extent that their self-esteem plummets drastically. Then, why do we do it to ourselves?

Starting today, for every negative thought you have about yourself, disrupt that pattern by thinking at least two to five good thoughts about yourself. Your good thoughts about yourself have to be at least doubled. Everyone has beautiful qualities that Allah has granted to all of us so don't try to take the temporary easy road out by thinking that there are no good qualities in you. Allah is far more generous and kind beyond understanding, and He has extended much of His generosity towards you.

All seemingly negative situations have countless good in them, but we don't know the unseen, so we tend to have a very limited understanding about the entirety of the situation, and that is one of the reasons we dwell in negativity. Inshallah keep a journal or a paper with you to remind you of your good qualities whenever you begin to think negatively about yourself. Having a mental list is helpful as well, but it is better if you have it written and you can read it out loud to yourself. You can read your list at any time: before an exam, an interview, a speech or any stressful situation. Read your list of good qualities about yourself even if you are not in a stressful situation, because reminding yourself of who you are will bring a smile to your face and help you continue feeling positive about yourself.

Is Anything Possible?

I don't know if everything is possible, but I believe that almost anything is possible in terms of our abilities that Allah has given us as human beings. People have reached the moon, yet we still doubt ourselves and think that the kind of life we would like for ourselves is *impossible* for us to have. By now, we should remove this word from our vocabulary, because we do have a certain amount of control over what we choose to do and how we choose to live our lives.

Understanding that almost anything is possible can be really motivating and empowering, allowing us to really test the limits of the barriers and boundaries we have imposed upon ourselves. Let us free ourselves from the shackles we have chained ourselves to and begin to benefit massively from this belief. You can achieve whatever goals you have by believing that it is possible and begin to work towards them diligently and consistently.

People have pushed through every kind of impossibility. For example, a person may get into a car accident and end up paralyzed. The doctors tell him his paralysis is permanent. That would be devastating, to say the least. Yet, with his thoughts alone, he refuses to believe the doctor and works on his mindset, believing he can walk again, and he does! Read about neuroplasticity and people who have endured heartbreaking setbacks, and yet rose above it all stronger and better.

After all, there is a cure for everything. However, it doesn't just apply to your health; it applies to any aspect of your life. What is incredible is knowing that you can change your future by your thoughts alone, with complete trust and devotion to Allah. As soon as you know this, you can begin to work on whatever it is that you want to achieve.

No difficulty or obstacle is greater than Allah. As Muslims, we don't like to attribute negativity to Allah, but we know that everything comes from Him, The Exalted. Therefore, just as Allah created any obstacle or hardship, He can also remove it from us. However, if we want the immediate help of Allah, we must remember Him. Allah says in the Quran chapter 2, verse 152, in a close translation, "So, remember me, I will remember you."

With Allah by your side, nothing is impossible. He showed Jannah to the magicians who accepted Islam in the time of the Prophet Musa, peace be upon him, in their prostration. Allah showed Asiya, peace be upon her, the wife of Pharaoh, her house in Jannah when she made dua to Allah. Allah gave Dhul Qarnayn the ability to build an iron wall between two mountains, and till this day, the Yajuj and Majuj are kept away from destroying us alhumdulillah.

Allah made an illiterate shepherd a prophet, blessed him with the inheritance of the best and biggest following and nation, and raised his name above every other creation. He was Prophet Muhammad, may Allah bestow peace and blessings upon our beloved messenger, who was given the gift and miracle of being ascended to the heavens on the night journey. He was an orphan from a place unheard of and yet he was raised to such a status that no human being had ever reached nor will ever reach. This is how Allah chooses to bless and provide for His servants.

Inshallah all we have to do is worship Allah. Praise His praises and believe that He is there to help us. Nothing is hard for Him, and He can do whatever He wills. He is always available to us, never tiring in the least. Give yourself to Allah's worship, and you will see miracles abound in both of your worlds inshallah, because nothing is impossible.

Face Challenges Head On

People have a variety of fears. Oftentimes, it limits our potential and hinders us from excelling. The fear of anything can be overwhelming or even paralyzing.

Most of us have something we fear. We are afraid of failure or we fear being successful. We are afraid to try something new for fear of looking unintelligent or we avoid promising goals out of fear of having to work hard or face uncertainty. We are afraid of rejection and working towards goals that are meaningful to us. We are afraid of removing ourselves from our comfort zones, and so we end up not trying at all.

There are many paths to dealing with fear. My way of dealing with fear is to just do it. Whatever it is that makes me afraid, I face it head on. I can deal with the outcome, but I cannot deal with the increasing anxiety, as I continue to avoid the task at hand. I'm sure many people make it worse for themselves by thinking and worrying about whatever it is they have to do, rather than actually doing it and getting started. Once you get started, you realize, "Hey, it's not that bad. This is actually easy." So, like Nike, just do it.

Stay in the Present

Most of us are usually lost in our thoughts, either thinking about past events or thinking about the future. We replay in our minds over and over certain negative situations that took place or we do the opposite, always daydreaming or worried about the future, failing to realize that it may never materialize. Constant rummaging through our past and future costs us our present, which is all we really have. Sometimes, a single moment is all we have.

Negative thought processes can result in discontentment and utter unhappiness with life. This can also lead to depression, which is devastating. I have been increasingly seeing this in young Muslims. They are so worried about situations that took place in their past and, at the same time, they have an almost paralyzing fear of the future. Mostly, young people are worried about their careers, marriage, and whether they will be successful or not. So they continue the endless mind-numbing circle of negative thoughts.

It is not necessarily a bad thing to reflect about our past in a healthy manner. We can learn from our past mistakes and make conscious choices to be better inshallah, while thinking about the future is an Islamic quality, and it is a necessary part of life. However, the problem arises when we dwell in negative thoughts about the past or have worries about the future that turn to anxiety and fear. That's when we really need to rethink our thoughts, and find ways to live in the present. What's ironic is that our future is directly dependent on what we do now, in the moment.

So, how do we stop ourselves when we are plunged into such negative thoughts?

The pointers below will help clarify how we can live in the moment and stay present inshallah. These tips aren't in any specific order, so you can apply whichever ones you would like to first or last.

Realize that All We Have is the Present Moment

The past is gone, and the future may never come. This realization alone can be enough to immediately center our thoughts and break the habit of thinking negatively. Although it requires practice again and again, it can be done. And when you do, you will be so thankful.

Remember Your Reasoning

Think about what you are doing and why you are doing it. If those thoughts you were lost in were not meaningful, bring yourself right back to the present and stay there. This is because if such thoughts are not meaningful to you or in line with your goals for yourself, then you might as well do away with them. We do not have time to waste, because we, by design, are an elevated creation, and we must be respectful of that and hold ourselves in high esteem. So, when you think deeply about it, you will realize whether it is worth your time or not. When you realize what is meaningful to you, eliminate all of that which is not.

Do Less

When you have less things to do on your list of goals to accomplish for the day, you feel less overwhelmed. Then you can actually focus on the most important things to be done during the day. Usually, it's one or two things that are the most time-consuming and yet the most important. So, focus your energy on those tasks, and be mindful of your thoughts.

Live Each Moment Deliberately

Do it on purpose. Whatever it is that we decide to do, we must do it because we want to, not because during the course of the day, time just ran out, and that's how things just happened to be. It rarely happens like that, because we make the choice to let it happen that way. Now, some things are not in our power, and we accept that as Muslims, but there is so much that we do have control over. We have been given amazing abilities to make those choices. So, the next time your mind wanders, decide that you will stay in the present and live in the moment.

Breathe

The power of taking a deep breath is phenomenal. If you notice, the answer is usually in all of the simple things, most of which you already possess, like breathing. It is totally free and relaxing. When you are overwhelmed and feel like your mind is racing through too many jumbled thoughts, just take a deep breath and then come back to live in the moment.

Some people meditate, and I have done it too, but I find salah (prayer), dua, and Quran recitation to be even more soothing and relaxing, all of which has helped me stay in the present and appreciate life.

Stay Present in Conversations

When having a conversation with someone, listen and stay in the moment with them. Don't just think about what you want to say next and have answers lined up before they even finish their sentence. You can learn a lot from people by just listening to them. Some people have gone through a wealth of experience and have so much wisdom we can learn from. So, just listen and appreciate what the person is really saying, verbally and non-verbally.

Stop Worrying About the Future

InshaAllah whatever is meant to be, it will be. We cannot make the future come any faster nor can we delay it. That, however, does not mean that you don't plan and work hard to achieve the goals you have for yourself. Rather, it is an acceptance of all that which we do not have control over. What we do have control over is the present. So let the future go and focus on living in the moment.

Make Dua

Like the recitation of Quran, heartfelt dua is one of the greatest experiences any person can ever have. There are many duas that our Prophet Mohammad, peace be upon him, did, and they are all-encompassing. They include anything and everything mashallah. You can learn to read duas from Sheikh Yasir Qadhi's book, *Dua: Weapon of the Believer*. You can also buy *Fortress of the Muslim*, which scholars love and speak highly about.

You can also make a list of all of the duas specific to you, in any language. Ask Allah to help you and the rest of us live in the moment and stay present to truly appreciate life inshallah.

Reflect about Creation and Your Surroundings

When you are driving, look up at the sky and notice what a pretty blue it is. When it rains, notice the beautiful clouds and the fresh mornings, and how it gives life to everything around us. Think about the trees and how beautifully green and strong they are, and especially how bright a green they are right after it rains and when the sun comes out. Think about your feet in the sand at the beach, and feel the sand through your toes.

These are all moments that can help you appreciate the present. Reflecting about creation has changed people's lives, and I am one of those people. It has even made them embrace Islam. When you think about Allah's creation, you realize that no entity or being could have made any of it, except for Allah. So, knowing that there is a Creator out there watching over you and providing for you will inshallah make you feel better, stay positive, and increase your appreciation for life.

Don't Compare Yourself to Others

Don't think about the grass being greener on the other side. It rarely ever is, if at all. When we stop thinking about other people's lives, we realize the extraordinary ability to make our lives whatever it is that we want it to be. We have been given the ability to choose, and this realization alone, too, can help us live in the present and live meaningful lives.

Refrain from judging your own life harshly and becoming unsatisfied as a result of what you see in other people's lives, especially on social media, because that is not reality. When people choose to share online that which gives off the false impression that their lives are filled with excitement, adventure, and ease, don't be so quick to feel negative about your own life. We should be more than happy when someone out there is free of hardships and afflictions, and seems like he or she has it together. At the same time, however, we should realize that those are only moments displayed on a screen, and it is not the whole picture. We only see what the people choose to put online for us to see. There is so much more that might be going on behind the scenes that if we knew, it would cause us to appreciate our own lives more.

People go through all kinds of hardships like terrible car accidents that leave them in chronic pain, heartbreaking divorces, death, and/or low self-esteem issues that they might be struggling with. But people are not necessarily going to put that online for you and the world to see so that everyone could have an accurate picture of what really goes on in their lives. So, be grateful for the grass being greener on your side, and don't look at what other people have. Allah even advised the Prophet Mohammad, peace be upon him, not to turn his eyes towards what others had in the enjoyment of the world. In the Quran, chapter 15, verse 88, Allah says, "Do not strain your eyes (longingly) towards what we have given to certain classes of them as enjoyment." This verse advised Prophet Mohammad, peace be upon him, not to be concerned with what the disbelievers had of worldly benefits. Our enjoyment, as believers, lies in the hereafter so we should not turn our eyes to what anyone else has, especially it if will cause us to become unappreciative of what we have already been given by Allah.

As you keep practicing these habits, you will notice a higher appreciation for even the smallest things in your life. You will come to cherish small moments that at one point you may have overlooked and deemed unimportant. However, with the consistent practice of any of the above points I mentioned, you are well on your way to being more present, living in the moment, and improving your ability to think positively. In the long run, the implementation of these actions will contribute tremendously to achieving a Muslim mindset inshallah.

Lesson 7:
Wake Up Early

THE habit of waking up early is one of the best Islamic habits I have ever learned. Successful, impactful, and influential people wake up early. The tranquility and calmness of the morning is one the most perfect times to practice sincerity and concentration in your prayer, to be creative, exercise, or just soak in the morning freshness.

Waking up early, preferably before Fajr, is an important step in achieving a Muslim mindset, and it can help you can make other Islamic practices a habit during this time to help strengthen your eman, and remain positive and optimistic. It is the best time to put everything in perspective, and it determines the flow of the rest of your day.

Waking up early gives you a head start on your goals while others are still sleeping. Waking up early will make it easier for you to recite Quran, make dua, and do dhikr in solitude. Strive very hard to make waking up early a habit so that you can achieve the same positive mindset of influential and optimistic people. You will see the fruits of your efforts, and Allah will reward you immensely inshallah. As stated in Riyad Al-Saliheen, Prophet Mohammad, peace be upon him, said, "Blessings are in the early hours for my nation." It is then no wonder that in the mornings, we can get more done, because they are filled with blessings.

Needless to say, for people in the Western countries, waking up early is difficult to practice, because people go to sleep late and wake up even later. As Muslims, we have adopted this practice, and it is time we got back to the Sunnah and the way of our pious predecessors. To accomplish this, I have some pointers for you below to help you wake up early inshallah.

Prepare the Night Before

The preparation for knowing how to wake up early starts the day and night before. This is vital. So prepare the day before. On the day before, keep in mind that your goal is to wake up early the next morning, inshallah. With this thought in mind, get started on your to-do list as soon as possible. Yes, you should have a list of tasks that you need to do for the day. Your time is too valuable to just wander about and have it become wasted. I personally am not a fan of long to-do lists, because looking at a long list of things to do can cause more anxiety. What you can do is list the most important and necessary tasks first and do them right away. As long as you do these tasks, and even if you don't get to the rest of the list, your day will still feel productive inshallah.

Don't Let Everything Pile Up in the Evening

From what I have noticed, during the day, we tell ourselves we have enough time. Thus, we do all of the fun and unimportant tasks and put off the most important goals at the bottom of the list. This constant procrastination results in too many things to do at night, causing us to catch up on our to-do list late into the night, which further causes us to sleep late. So, get all of your important tasks done early in the day, and don't let things pile up.

Drink Your Tea or Coffee Early

Drink your tea or coffee early in the evening, preferably no later than 6:00, which some people would still consider as late. This applies to people who drink coffee and tea, so if you don't, be proud of yourself for not having to deal with this. Caffeine makes you stay up late, which for most people just means that they will end up wasting their time watching TV or scrolling through their Facebook or Twitter feeds. Really work on this habit, because some people are under the assumption that they are suffering from insomnia, when in actuality, if they were to not drink caffeine late at night, they would be fine.

Eat Dinner Early

This also ties into the idea of knowing beforehand, early in the day, what you will be doing that day. So, being aware of whether you have enough leftovers in the fridge or if you want to cook again today are important and time-consuming tasks, so you need to know the answers to them early on. That being said, when it is time to eat dinner, eat at a reasonable time so that by the time you go to sleep, you are not hungry again, causing you to get a late-night snack or a whole other dinner! Aim for eating at least three to four hours before you have to be asleep. This is an important practice, because when you sleep on a full stomach, the acid in the stomach regurgitates into the esophagus (food tube) and, over time, it erodes away the tissue. This is called heartburn. Oftentimes, if this condition persists for a long time, it leads to cancer, and many other problems.

Set an Alarm

Inshallah, one day we will reach a stage where we are no longer in need of an alarm, but for the time being, use it. Here is what I will share with you about setting alarms so you can wake up early: you have to know how much sleep you specifically need.

Let's say that you need at least seven hours of sleep, otherwise you will be sleepy and tired all day. Maybe you are just starting out and working on waking up early. You decide that you want to wake up at 6 in the morning. If you know that the amount of sleep you need is at least seven hours, then you want to be asleep by 11 at night—not just getting into bed at 11 p.m., but actually being asleep at that time. You should be in bed at least fifteen minutes before to allow yourself enough time to fall asleep by 11 p.m.

Keep Your Alarm Far Away

Keep it so far away from you that the only way to turn it off is for you to get out of bed and walk to it. Keep it across the room. Make sure that you set the most irritating sound for your alarm, so that it makes you jump out of bed and turn it off. It works wonders.

Wake Up at the Same Time Every Day

Don't confuse your body's rhythm by waking up at different hours all the time. Accustom yourself to wake up at the same time so that you can sleep well, be refreshed in the morning, and wake up early.

Once You Wake Up, Stay Up

One of the best actions to take when waking up early is to keep the momentum. Do something that forces you to keep your eyes open and makes you want to stay up. Turn on the lights and open the curtains so that it is very bright in your sleeping headquarters. Try exercising, jumping rope, or drinking water or tea. Do anything that keeps you awake—only halal things, of course.

Have Someone Else Wake You Up

Having others wake you up helps tremendously, especially if you know they are early birds. This one is a big help, because others' support encourages you to not disappoint them, and holds you accountable. A very important thing to keep in mind here is that you remind yourself that they are just trying to help you and are making it easier for you to accomplish your goal, because you will be very irritated and annoyed of them. So remain patient and let them know you appreciate their help.

Plan an Activity

Have a meaningful and fun activity planned for the next morning so that getting up makes you excited. For example, plan to go to the beach in the early morning with a friend. The beach is beautiful in the morning; it is so calm and serene. Just thinking about it will make you happy. So, think of any meaningful and simple activity that will make you excited about getting up, then go ahead and actually do it.

Relax Before Sleep

Do a meaningful and relaxing activity the night before. Take a warm shower, or stretch. Do your bedtime adhkar, the remembrance of Allah. This should fill you heart with trust and reliance upon Allah. It will fill your heart with peace and tranquility inshallah.

Say Salam to Everyone

Give salam to your loved ones before going to bed. You might not wake up at all the next day. Life is short, and as Muslims, we must always keep the end in mind. Our true home is waiting for us in

Jannah inshallah. If the last memory your family has of you is that you embraced them and said salam to them, then it is a very beautiful way to be remembered.

Dim the Lights

This tricks the body into thinking that it's time to sleep, so you will naturally feel tired. You should also turn off all of your electronics. Using electronics late into the night will lead to having more sleep problems. So, resist the urge and turn them off. Keep them far away from you, so you are not tempted.

Forgive Anyone and Everyone

Sometimes, people toss and turn and stay awake several hours into the night, because they are hurting and stressed. This makes them wake up groggy and tired the next morning, causing them to push back their goal to wake up early. So, resolve to forgive everyone. No one is worth missing your salah over the next morning. Whatever problems you had yesterday will most likely be there the next day, so train yourself to let it go, and you will feel the weight of a mountain lifting off of you.

Make Dua to Wake Up Early

This really works alhumdulillah, and why wouldn't it work? Allah never rejects dua (supplication). Make dua to wake up on time for your salah, especially on days when you lose your charger or if you suspect that your phone will die during the night, and this is only if you use your phone as an alarm. I am mentioning this towards the end of this section, because it is necessary that you do your part first, and then ask Allah for help. This follows the idea of tying your camel first, then putting your trust in Allah. So, do all of the other actions that I mentioned above first, then pray to Allah.

Be Patient with Yourself

Give yourself time to become accustomed to the new schedule. Start gradually, and implement any of the steps one at a time. Gradual progress is long-term progress. Trying to change overnight is not a lasting change, although there are rare instances of success that some may have experienced. If you falter, don't be hard on yourself. Just start again the next day.

Also, try your best not to wake up by a whole 1-3 hours before your usual wake-up time. Try waking up by increments of 10-15 minutes. Then, when you feel like you have a firm grasp on waking up at that time, wake up earlier by another 10-15 minutes until you reach your desired goal. Before you know it, all of your hard work will pay off and you will feel so much better about yourself. Your self-confidence, self-esteem, and productivity will go up and you will feel like a better version of yourself inshallah.

I have experimented with almost all of the points I have mentioned above and have gotten better at waking up early. Give any of them a try inshallah, and hopefully you can become an early bird too.

I spent a lot of time talking specifically about waking up early, because it is instrumental in achieving a Muslim mindset. We must take advantage of the blessings that descend during the early hours. Practice the tips mentioned in this lesson, and work hard to make this powerful habit of waking up early a daily routine in your life.

Lesson 8:
Practice Gratitude Daily

MAKE gratitude a regular practice in your life. If I could think of anything that would ensure a meaningful life other than our belief in the existence of Allah, it is gratitude.

The people who are at peace and enjoy contentment in their lives are those who practice gratitude. The successful ones are those who are grateful for the small and big aspects of life. We will never really enjoy life unless we first begin to appreciate and become grateful for what we have already been blessed with. You can spend your whole life searching for meaning and happiness but never come across any of it, because you may not have learned how to appreciate it even when it was right in front of you.

Gratitude is a prophetic practice and a character gem. No human has ever or will ever endure and suffer more than our beloved guides who came before to guide humanity back to the straight path as the prophets have. If we are to follow any example in our lives so that we may understand what life truly means, it is their example we must follow. One of their examples was gratitude.

In our American culture, some of us are taught to embrace the future and prepare for it to such an extent that we ignore the present. We are indirectly taught to chase success to such an extent that we begin to have anxiety about our current conditions. We are taught to chase money, and we are pressured to make the amount of money we amass to boost our self-worth, as though there is nothing more important in life than having lots of wealth. It is no wonder that we have anxiety and depression as our lifestyle. It is unnatural to the Muslim to find complete peace and tranquility in anything other than in nearness to Allah.

We need to slow down. We must stop and appreciate the fleeting gifts of life, time, good health, relationships, and the desire for knowledge, all of which are given to us for free. Were these gifts to be taken away, they could not be acquired through wealth. They are gifts from Allah, and we must draw in nearness to Allah, the only One worthy of all praise.

We must be grateful for the little things in life as well. Every little or big thing is worthy of gratitude. Big things don't happen in our lives regularly, so find pleasure in small wins and small things. Every day is a blessing and an opportunity to be greater than we were yesterday.

Every moment and every breath is something to be awestruck by for which we are forever indebted to our Creator. It is true what Allah said— that were we to count the blessings bestowed upon us, we would never be able to.[15] Think about that for a moment. This statement includes all people and creations. Every single person has been given so much that he would never be able to count it all, because its quantity is beyond our capacity to calculate or even fathom.

So, how can we then be ungrateful? We are the most gifted and beloved creation. How can we then forsake our current blessings and be anxious about that which may never even take place?

We may never find true meaning and purpose if we don't find even a few moments in our day to be grateful for what we already have in our lives. Therefore, adopt this prophetic practice of gratitude. Look for the good in every situation, even though there may be no good apparent in it to you.

---

[15] Quran 14:34

Every day, before or after salah, be grateful for even one thing, and say it to yourself out loud. When you wake up in the morning, be grateful for being given yet another day to live and experience the beauty of life. Be grateful that the sun rose from the east and that you witnessed its rising. Reflecting about the sun, or any other creation helps you to understand life in profound ways. Make a practice of it and you will see its benefits, and inshallah it will be a means of further guidance for you.

Allah said, "If you are grateful to me, I will surely increase you."[16] If you are grateful, you will be given more. This is the sunnah of our Creator. This is who He is. He doesn't deprive nor does He make His servant suffer. Instead, He wants to reward you and give you more. So, become more grateful to Allah and He will provide even more for you.

If we want to achieve more and have what we do not have, we must become grateful for what we already have. This is important for achieving goals, because as we are striving towards our goals, some of us become so focused on it or overwhelmed by it that we lose sight of all the beautiful gifts that Allah has already given to us.

---

[16] Quran 14:7

You must hone the ability to recognize a gift when it has been given to you. You must recognize and be cognizant of the intent of the giver. In this case, the giver is Allah. You must learn to filter out all of the negativity and zoom in on the good and the blessings accompanied by the gift. We learned how to do that in the previous sections.

As you recognize the gift, return it with an even better gift. This is difficult to do with Allah, because nothing we do for Him is worth anything, nor should it ever be compared to what He does for us. However, it can be applied to people and our relationships. We can give them more than they give us, and show excitement and happiness with the gifts they gave us. This is one way of responding to the giver of the gift. Utilize the gift the way it was intended. So, don't break or toss the gift aside if someone gave it to you; rather, we should use it and show them that we are grateful for it.

We can show Allah that we are grateful by using our limbs, organs, and abilities in a way that He intended. We should keep ourselves away from sins and use the gifts Allah bestowed upon us in a way that is pleasing to Him.

Being grateful is good for you, and its practice will never bring you any negativity. In the tafsir of Ibn Kathir, Abu Qatada said that a blessing that you are grateful for could never harm you. So inshallah make a habit of being grateful and be amazed by its results.

Gratitude is contagious. When you adopt this prophetic practice, it will affect those around you as well. They, too, will become more grateful, and life won't seem so bad anymore. Life will begin to change for all of you. In fact, you will become excited and look forward to the coming day instead of awaiting it anxiously or feeling like you want to crawl back into your bed.

So, what are you grateful for?

Every day you should mention a few things out loud that you are grateful for. We, Muslims, usually practice this when making dua, but it also helps to set up a certain time for it. Morning is the perfect time to do this or when you are going to sleep. Just take five minutes to practice gratitude, and soon enough, it will be a part of you and you will almost always find yourself being in a state of "gratefulness."

Narrations of Gratitude

Below are some narrations to help supplement the importance of gratitude.

In Riyad Al-Salihen, Abu Hurayrah, Allah be pleased with him, narrated that the Prophet, peace be upon him said, "Richness is not in the abundance of wealth, rather it is self-sufficiency."

This is a very critical narration, because it highlights the importance of being independent of asking or begging people for anything. Self-sufficiency can be achieved by being content and grateful for what Allah has already granted to us, and not turn our eyes towards what other people have. We should submit to whatever provisions Allah chooses to give us and be more than happy with them. This hadith does not mean that we should stop striving in earning and working hard, rather we should accept graciously whatever Allah gives us as a result of our efforts.

Another similar narration Imam Nawawi mentioned is that Abdullah ibn Amr ibn Al-As, may Allah be pleased with him, reported that the Prophet, peace be upon him, said, "Successful is the one who has entered the fold of Islam and is provided with sustenance which is sufficient for his needs, and Allah makes him content with what He has bestowed upon him." We learn a few things from this hadith. One of the first points to consider is that contentment comes from Allah. Therefore, we should ask Allah to make us content and grateful with whatever He bestows upon us. We should make dua for self-sufficiency, and become happy and at peace with whatever resources we have, even if we feel that they are limited.

Practicing contentment leads to humility and submission to the Will of Allah, because He gives us without any measure and without even asking for it. It is virtuous to be grateful and to appreciate everything we have, even if it is less than what others have. It is even more virtuous when a rich man is grateful and content with what Allah has given him.

Ibn Masud, may Allah be pleased with him, narrated that the Messenger of Allah, peace be upon him, said, "Envy is permitted only in two cases: a man whom Allah gives wealth, and he disposes of it rightfully, and a man to whom Allah gives knowledge, which he applies and teaches."[17]

Something to consider about this hadith is that it is permissible for Muslims to be wealthy; therefore, we should not fear success in terms of money. Another thing to consider is that we are normally advised against being envious of anyone, but it has been allowed in the case of a person who is wealthy, but spends his wealth in the right way. This type of envy is a form of wishing to have what someone else has without wishing evil to befall the envied person or for his wealth to be taken away from him or her.

The wealthy person's spending of his money and resources is a way for him to show gratitude

---

[17] Al-Nawawi, 217-218.

to Allah as is the imparting of knowledge to others for the one who has been blessed with it. This practice of spending your wealth in the right way or benefiting others with the knowledge given to us falls under the concept of showing gratitude to Allah by using the gift in the way it was intended.

The person who showed gratitude in the best way and the most sincerely was none other than our Prophet Mohammad, peace be upon him. Imam Nawawi mentions the hadith of Aisha, may Allah be pleased with her, when she narrated that the Prophet, peace be upon him, would stand in prayer so long that his feet would swell. She asked him, "Why do you do this when Allah has forgiven your future and past sins?" He said, "Should I not be a grateful slave of Allah?"

From this hadith, we learn about the humility and gratitude the Prophet, peace be upon him, practiced. He never faltered in thanking Allah or in recognizing the blessings bestowed upon him. He is the best example for us to follow, not just in knowing how to be grateful, but rather, in every aspect of our lives.

This hadith also teaches us that the more we have been gifted and granted by Allah, the more we should reciprocate His kindness to us with as much gratitude as possible on our part. The best form of gratitude to Allah is in worshipping Him with extra prayers and acts of worship after having fulfilled the commandments.

Gratitude is the key to a fulfilling life. The more we are grateful, the more we are given. Gratitude leads to our happiness and corrects any negativity we may have within us. It fills us with joy and makes us appreciate everything we already have. It affects our mindset positively more than any pill will.

Gratitude makes us more creative, helps us bounce back faster from any hardship we may have endured, and helps us have better social relationships. Gratitude does not necessarily mean that we think life is great all of the time or that we don't have problems. Gratitude simply recognizes how blessed we are, even in the midst of a storm.

I hope that you see by now how vital gratitude is to our lives. The main point to take away from this chapter is to practice gratitude daily, and to be appreciative of what you already have, especially if you seek more and want more. Also, the more we are given, the more we should be grateful. By practicing gratitude, and keeping in mind the example and narrations of our prophets, peace be upon them, inshallah we will find it easier to attain a Muslim Mindset.

Lesson 9:
Strive Towards Patience

MANY people have most likely heard that patience is a virtue. I believe most people don't understand what patience really means. I didn't really understand what it meant to be patient myself until I began to face difficulties upon difficulties. I think there is so much more patience to attain and hopefully even master one day inshallah.

One of the first things we should do when we are faced with difficulties or uncertainty in life is to practice patience. The praiseworthiness of patience is too great to even enumerate. I have seen scholars and elders advise people again and again to keep steadfast upon patience, even when you might wonder what does patience have to do with this? However, patience has a lot to do with everything. So, what is patience?

In Arabic, the word for patience is sabr. In *Nadhra An-Naim,* we learn that sabr means to stop or withhold one's self. When you face difficulties, be they of any type or magnitude, you should stop yourself, or withhold yourself. In Islam, patience is divided into three categories: sabr with sins, sabr with facing difficulties, and sabr with obedience to Allah.

When we are faced with a sinful situation, we display patience by stopping ourselves from getting involved in the sin in the first place. We work hard, day and night, to avoid going near any sins. This practice of refraining from sins is patience, and it is immensely rewarding in both lives.

The other type of patience I mentioned is having patience with difficulties. I have never met a person who didn't have difficulties in their lives, whether they mentioned it or not. Observation alone is an incredible tool in recognizing people's hardships, and making dua for them so that they may be alleviated of it.

Difficulties can be of all types, and they can be such that people become so hopeless that they stop believing in Allah altogether. This is a lack of sabr. When you have difficulties, which most of us do, we do what we can to alleviate ourselves of them, and we leave the rest to Allah. We have to stop ourselves from crossing boundaries we are not supposed to even tread near as believers. Difficulties are trying for many of us, and they test us to limits that were previously unknown to us. However, we must not give up, and we must keep forging ahead. As Muslims, we must always have hope. We must have faith that Allah will relieve us of our hardships and that ease will prevail.

In the Quran, chapter 95, verses 4-5, we are informed that, verily, with every hardship comes ease—and not just one ease, but two eases. The ease doesn't come after the hardship as some might think; rather, it comes alongside the hardship. Therefore, whenever you are faced with difficulties, look for the ease. It is there. It will protect you from feeling overwhelmed, and it will help you build a mindset of strength and resilience.

The last type of patience is patience with obedience to Allah. There are certain commandments we must fulfill as Muslims. They include the five daily prayers; the other pillars of Islam; dutifulness and kindness to parents and relatives; and fulfilling the rights of anyone who may have rights over us.

Obedience requires patience. There are certain obligations that we as Muslims must adhere to and fulfill to their fullest extent. That requires immense amount of patience. Praying five times a day requires so much patience that you actually see yourself having to give up other things in order to fulfill this right of Allah. We must schedule our entire lives around prayers, and at times, it is not that easy. If it were easy, everyone would be doing it. It requires discipline, sacrifice, and most importantly, sincerity. Any act of worship requires sincerity, which can be very difficult for all of us, as Shaitan works very diligently to lead us astray and to divert us from maintaining concentration and focus.

Praying, fasting during the month of Ramadan, giving zakat (obligatory charity), hajj, wearing a hijab, as well as many of the other acts of worship require high levels of patience, and stopping yourself from other worldly aspirations, and remaining steadfast like a pillar upon obedience to Allah. If we are to succeed in having patience in all of the above-mentioned aspects of our lives, we will transform not only ourselves, but also the world as a whole inshallah.

Read and learn about the lives of our pious predecessors and reflect about their contributions to the world. They were out-of-this-world kind of people.

Patience is a virtue. When we harness the ability to forbear all difficulties, we grow as people and become that much closer to achieving our fullest potential, and becoming whole. We draw in nearness to our Creator, and we enjoy a higher quality of life. Our mindsets begin to change and move further in the spectrum of positivity, and our hearts become peaceful. No longer will we be chained by fears of the unknown. No longer will we accept anxiety and depression as a lifestyle. We will dwell in tranquility and serenity.

Some people might think of patience as passive acceptance or weakness. Both are incorrect interpretations of this magnificent virtue. Patience is active. It requires you to actively control your thoughts and fight day in and day out the negativity that, at times, feels insurmountable. Patience requires active effort on one's part to endure life's most difficult circumstances and persevere through them, even if it takes decades or a whole lifetime. Now, we can put to rest any inclination we may have towards perceiving patience as weakness or passive. Patience is beautiful, and it makes life even more beautiful.

The Virtues of Patience

The number of verses from the Quran and narrations from the Prophet, peace be upon him, extolling us towards patience and perseverance are many. They highlight the necessity and importance of patience in almost all aspects of our lives.

Allah says in the Quran, chapter 2, verse 155, "And indeed, we will test you with something of fear, hunger, loss of wealth, lives and fruits, but give glad tidings to those who are patient." I am always touched by this verse, because poverty, loss of loved ones and fear is something that many of us face in our lives. Allah states very clearly that we will be tested greatly, and that difficulties will be a part of our lives in this world. The solution Allah puts forward is that we should be patient. The ones who are patient are given glad tidings, because they persevere and remain grateful to Allah no matter what the circumstances are.

In a narration reported by Abu Malik Al-Harith bin Asim, may Allah be pleased with him, the Prophet, peace be upon him, said, "Patience is light."[18] Patience and perseverance are praiseworthy character traits of the believers and the pious predecessors whom we try to emulate. Patience is necessary for all successful people, because without patience, it would not be possible to endure life's hardships and failures. We must hone the ability to remain patient when life does not turn out the way we had intended and attain its light.

Allah will reward us and elevate us for any pain or suffering we endure in this life by forgiving

---

[18] Al-Nawawi, 34.

our sins. Regarding this, Abu Sa'id and Abu Hurayrah, may Allah be pleased with them both, reported that the Prophet, peace be upon him, said, "Never is a believer stricken with a discomfort, an illness, an anxiety, a sadness, a grief, or worry, or harm, or even the pricking of a thorn but that Allah will expiate his sins on account of his patience."[19]

This hadith is truly profound, and it shows the significance of Allah's mercy and grace. Allah not only forgives our sins for the major hardships and sufferings of life, but even the pricking of a thorn. We should note that anything we endure, even something as much as an atom's weight of discomfort, Allah is already aware of it and will forgive our sins because of it. This only happens if we remain patient and persevere, which can be done by refraining from complaining or blaming others, including Allah.

To further explain the significance of patience, Abu Hurayrah, may Allah be pleased with him, narrated that the Messenger, peace be upon him, said, "He whom Allah intends good for, Allah afflicts him with some affliction (hardship)." [20] I don't want us to think that Allah is somehow out to get us, because our afflictions are a source of

---

[19] Al-Nawawi, 39.
[20] Al-Nawawi, 40.

mercy from Allah to us. It may be that we are moving further and further away from Allah in our lives, and He does not wish for us to be distanced from Him, so Allah, out of His love for us, afflicts us with some difficulty so that we might turn to Him for help and aid. Therefore, hardships are a natural part of our lives, but patience is something we must actively work towards attaining.

Abu Yahya Suhaib bin Sinan, may Allah be pleased with him, reported that the Messenger of Allah, peace be upon him, said, "How wonderful is the case of a believer; there is good for him in everything and this applies only to a believer. If prosperity attends him, he expresses gratitude to Allah, and that is good for him, and if adversity befalls him, he endures it patiently and that is better for him."[21] As believers, every condition is good for us, be it in good times or in difficulties. In good times, we should practice gratitude, and in hardships, we should practice patience. We should ask Allah for patience, and strive to be counted among those who are patient.

The Prophet, peace be upon him, said that "Whoever wants to be patient, Allah will give him patience, and no one is given a gift better and more comprehensive than patience."[22] We can

---

[21] Al-Nawawi, 35.
[22] Al-Nawawi, 35.

understand and learn patience from the stories of the Prophets, and of them Yaqoob, peace be upon him, is one who is prominently known for his patience. His son, Yousef, peace be upon him, was taken from him as a child, and thrown into the bottom of a well, and as a result of his grief at the loss of his son, he became blind. When Yaqoob, peace be upon him, was informed of the loss of his son, he responded by saying that he would practice "beautiful patience," (Quran 12:18).

However, in His all-encompassing wisdom, Allah returned Yousef, peace be upon him, to his father not just as the King of Egypt but as a prophet as well. This is how Allah chooses to reward those who practice beautiful patience, and the reward for patience is nothing less than Jannah (paradise).

From the above Quran verses and narrations, we begin to understand the importance and necessity of patience, be it in any affliction or hardship. We should strive to persevere and remain patient in all difficulties and adversities. Through the implementation of patience, we become closer to Allah, and secure a place for ourselves in Paradise inshallah.

Keep the verses of the Quran and the narrations in mind as you strive towards becoming more patient in dealing with sins, difficulties and obedience to Allah. Patience is a big part of achieving a Muslim mindset. Therefore, we must strive to make patience a part of our habits and character, because life is not without problems or difficulties. As you work diligently to have sabr, meaningfulness in life becomes more visible and a Muslim mindset more easily graspable.

Lesson 10: Execute Your Goals

NOW that you know what it means to have a Muslim mindset and believe that it is possible for you too, it's time to put it into practice. This is the last step and the most important step after correcting our beliefs. Without action, it is difficult to achieve our fullest potential as Muslims and as human beings. There is one saying that has forever touched my heart, and it states:

> "If you could envision the type of person God intended you to be, you would rise up and never be the same again."
>
> Anonymous

This quotation replays itself over and over in my head, challenging me to constantly improve and develop myself. Think about this saying and figure out what it means to you. Then figure out what you are meant to do in this life. The first step is to believe in Allah and then to do all the acts of worship that are fard, an obligation, upon you. Then, think about what it is that you were meant to achieve and accomplish in this life. What is your vision for yourself? This task can seem daunting at first, but inshallah I have some tips to help make the process simple.

The first thing to do is to purify our intentions, because intentions are more important than actions. All deeds are judged according to our intentions;[23] therefore, we want to make sure that our intentions are solely for Allah. His pleasure is all we seek, and for Him are all our sacrifices.

Now that you have taken a moment to purify your intentions, take action immediately. Step one is to implement all of the previous lessons I mentioned, one at a time. The idea here is to be consistent in adopting these lessons as a lifestyle. Consistency will have compounding effects. As I mentioned before, this means that the small steps you consistently take will add up over time to massive positive results.

Now, this is the fun part. If you already have a goal, and you know exactly what it is that you

---

[23] Al-Nawawi, 24.

would like to accomplish, then write it down. It can be a short-term goal or a long-term goal. As you write your main goal down, think about what you must do to accomplish it. What will be required of you to be successful in your goal?

Then write down the steps you have to take in order to achieve your goal. You can write them out as bullet points or in an outline format. Take some time to write your goals, and really think about them deeply, because you should want to spend your time working on meaningful goals only. Now that you have written the steps to achieve your goals, what sacrifices do you have to make in order to achieve them? All worthwhile and meaningful goals and aspirations require you to give up something in order to achieve them.

You may need to sacrifice some sleep and wake up earlier than you normally would. Maybe your goal will require you to eat less so that you can reach a certain weight or so that you can have more energy to study and worship Allah. You should realize that all successful people sacrifice something in order to enjoy a better future. They forsake their sleep, food, and even fun social activities in order to achieve success.

What are you willing to give up to achieve your goal? Make a firm intention, and write it down. This is an important step. You must know exactly what you have to give up in order to get what you want.

Remember to be intentional about everything you do from this point forward. You should know what you are doing, and more importantly, why you are doing it. If the answer somehow doesn't lead back to your goal being for the sake of Allah, renew your intentions. You have to be very clear about your reasons, and they must always be bigger than you are.

As human beings, we are not motivated for long by insignificant or meaningless tasks, which is why we feel empty sometimes when our lives are not congruent with what is meaningful to us. Once you have figured out what steps you have to take and what you are willing and ready to sacrifice to achieve your goals, get started on execution right away.

Take action immediately, and do not give up until your goal is accomplished. Work every single day on your goal, and if you falter, start over again and keep going.

Along the way, you will have many ups and downs. Some days, you will feel completely energized and unstoppable while the next day you won't even want to get out of bed. This is normal. However, you have to work through this and get your work done whether you feel like it or not. This attitude and habit will set you apart from millions of people who only take action when they feel like it and, as a result, accomplish less than their fullest potential. This is an important habit to acquire, because at this point in the book, we have learned to do away with mediocrity as a lifestyle. We will not accept anything less than our fullest potential.

Write down your goals every day. I write down my goals at least three times a day to remind myself, because we, by nature, are forgetful. So, write them down on a piece of paper or in a small journal, and carry it with you at all times. When you write your goals down, your mind begins to work on their execution subconsciously, even if you are not actively engaged in them.

The last step is to execute. Just do it. This is where the hard work and consistency comes into play. Whatever you want to do will not get done if you don't put in the work.

Get started with the most important work first as discussed previously. Surround yourself with people who can get you closer to your goal. Ask for your family's and your friends' support. If no one is there to support you, don't worry and just keep going. All you need is Allah anyway, and He will surround you with the people you need to help you inshallah.

Stay consistent and recognize when you have made progress. Be relentless in your efforts, and do not give up, no matter what. It will all be worth it in the end inshallah.

So, these are the steps for the person who already knows what he or she wants to do. But what about the people who want to make a positive impact on the world and have acquired the right mindset, but don't know where to begin?

If this applies to you, be at ease inshallah, because there is always a way. I have some guidelines that can help you figure out what to do and how to execute them as well.

How to Generate Ideas that Work for You

One of the most efficient and easiest ways to figure out an idea is to think about the problems you have. Is there a solution out there? Has the solution worked?

If you have a problem, find a solution for it. You can also get ideas by solving other people's problems. Try finding a solution to each problem and working towards them, researching, and seeking expert advice or even advice from family and friends. You will probably try out a few different ideas before finding the one that works for you. At times, this process can be frustrating and overwhelming, so remain patient with yourself.

You can try another method of finding ideas that can be a goal for you or even potentially profitable, depending on your intentions and whatever it is that you want to do. It's called "The 3 Ps." I first learned this from entrepreneur Pat Flynn. It is very helpful.

Write down seven things you are passionate about in one category, another seven things that are a problem for you or others, and another seven things that cause pain to you or others. The category of "pain" is actually the category of "fears" you have. For example, a "pain" category bullet point can include a fear of spiders or a fear of public speaking. A "problem" category can include, for example, not knowing how to make passive income or being unhappy with your current job. Now that you generally understand what the categories are, write down bullet points corresponding to each category.

Passion. Problem. Pain (fear).

Then narrow it down to three things that you are most interested in, and then of the three, pick only one.

Pick one first. Become a master at it. Learn everything you can about that one thing. You have to know more about it than anyone else, especially if you want to turn it into a business.

Many people have many different passions and goals that they want to achieve, and they are torn between what to choose. As frustrating as it is and as much uncertainty as it may cause you, for now, pick only one. There will come a time when you are able to follow other passions. And, not only that, you will also have the experience, the knowledge, the relationships, and the connections that you need in order to go on to the other ventures inshallah.

If you want to start a business and that is your goal, then following the ideas below will help you inshallah. Any of the steps I talk about in this book can be applied to any goal. If you want to memorize the Quran, start a blog, study Islam, start a business, or write a book, it can be applied to all of it inshallah.

So, let's get started. To figure out what to do, follow the advice of author and entrepreneur Brian Tracy. Get a piece of paper out and follow the guidelines I will share with you. I have done all of this myself in the past and found it to be very helpful.

Draw a Venn diagram. In the circle to the left, write out your passions, hobbies, interests, and skills. This is the circle of things that you care about and/or are good at. In the circle to the right, write the things that people care about and would be willing to pay you for. It can be products or services. It can be digital products or physical products, or services that you do for others that add value to their lives but something that you can profit from. It is halal; don't worry.

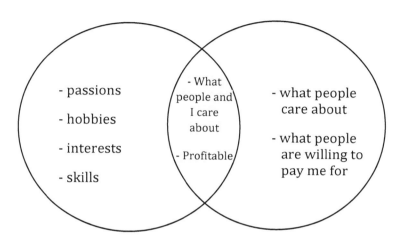

In the middle, where the circles intersect, is what you should focus on if you would like to start a business or if you just want to accomplish it as a goal, for profit or not. The intersection is where your skills, hobbies, and interests become aligned with products and services that people want and are willing to pay for. Then try out one thing at a time inshallah, and you will find what it is you are supposed to do. If at first you don't succeed, don't be hard on yourself. It wasn't meant to be. Just pick another and continue working on it inshallah.

What I have also done in the past is I made a list of goals and interests I have had and then picked the one that I knew I could do by myself without needing too many outside resources. Over time, as you do the above practices of the 3 Ps, the Venn diagram, and making lists, you will notice a pattern among them, and inshallah whatever you are meant to do will make itself apparent to you.

Do not reinvent the wheel. Surround yourself with mentors. Find someone who has done what you are trying to do and is successful at it. You would be amazed to find out how willing people are to pass on their knowledge and extend their help to you. Having mentors will help save you from a lot of hardships inshallah.

You can find mentors everywhere. There may be people in your family or community who can help you. I think the easiest place to find them is online. The world has changed dramatically in the last decade or so, and we now have access to more people and resources than ever before.

You could send them a private message on LinkedIn, Twitter or Facebook and then wait to see what happens. If you don't hear back from them, don't give up so easily. Be persistent and contact another, and be sincere in your interaction with people you look up to.

When you do get a mentor, follow their advice. It is probably one of the best ways you can repay them. Just do what they tell you and honor their time and help. Be diligent and hardworking. They cannot do the work for you; you have to put in the effort. Stay consistent, and persevere in every storm. If Allah has written it for you, you will get it inshallah. However, you will not know that until it actually happens, so keep moving forward.

Make sure you use good learning tactics. One of them was to find mentors. There are more. Go to seminars, read books about your goals daily, and watch and listen to audio programs and podcasts. There are many free tools available online, on YouTube, and other inexpensive programs on Amazon. Inshallah, Allah will open doors for you. Aim for mastery in your subject. Take baby steps, and do not overwhelm yourself by starting too big.

Make sure you get feedback that is constructive, knowledgeable, and trusted. Don't just get feedback from just anyone. Some people will hinder you more than they will help you, so know whom you are getting your feedback from. Remember the good companions.

Set a realistic deadline for yourself. This is a very important practice. When you give yourself a deadline, subconsciously your mind begins to prepare itself for that goal, and will work accordingly towards it. Don't give yourself too much time, especially if you know you can get it done in a shorter amount of time. You may have heard about Parkinson's Law[24], which states that work expands to fill the time allotted for it. So don't set a deadline of six months when you know that it can be done in three months nor should you set a deadline for a week when you know that it can be done in one day.

As you take action, work daily towards your goals, find mentors, and when you see that you are making progress, your mindset will begin to shift more rapidly. Action is one of the best ways to feel good about yourself. The wonderful thing about this is that most people have been given the abilities to really do anything they want in life.

As you notice that you are feeling better about yourself and you feel more confident in yourself and in your goals, keep the momentum going. This is the time to really push through and see what you're made of. You will be amazed at the abilities Allah has bestowed upon you.

Be relentless in your pursuits, especially those of the akhira (hereafter). Work harder than you have ever done before. It will all pay off very soon inshallah.

Have a daily, weekly, monthly and yearly checklist of your goals. Do something every day that moves you closer to your goals. Remind

---

[24] "Parkinson's Law," BrianTracy.com, Brian Tracy International, Web. 7 July 2017.

yourself every single day of what you set out to do and then do it. Ask for guidance and help from Allah and get your work done. If you face adversity on your journey to achieving your goals, pray and pray until you have achieved it, and always keep a positive outlook on every situation.

How to Stay Motivated

So, now you have a goal, maybe even several goals. Maybe you just started thinking about this or have had dreams of achieving it since a lifetime ago. You started your goal and then fell off the wagon, because you just couldn't motivate yourself enough to follow it through to the end.

You told yourself that instead of now, you will do it someday. "Someday, I will get that degree." "Someday I will travel to that country." "Someday I will start taking Arabic courses so I can understand the Quran." "Someday, I will build a masjid."

You are not alone. This happens all too often to many people. Most of us have goals and dreams we have been thinking about and have wanted to achieve, yet somehow, we have not found a way to actually do it. For many people, years pass by and *someday* never comes.

You may have even experienced bursts of motivation after reading this book, or after a conference, seminar, or Friday sermon, and you felt like you were on top of the world, and that you could do anything. Then as a day, week or month passed by, you were back to feeling sluggish and unmotivated.

So, how do we stay motivated? How can we keep the momentum going long after the initial spark of inspiration and feeling of empowerment has faded away?

There are many ways to stay motivated, but I have found the tips below to be the most helpful inshallah. I have stated some of these before, but they are all listed in points below.

Find Your Why

This is the first thing you should do. In order to stay motivated, you must figure out why it is that you have a certain goal. Your goals have to be meaningful to you, and they should not be goals that you can outgrow, especially for the long term.

What I mean by this is that our goals must transcend beyond worldly reasons. For example, we should not want to memorize the Quran or start a company just because we want to prove others wrong or show off to them. This kind of reasoning is not sustainable for long because once you achieve that goal, what then? You have already proven them wrong, so what will you do now?

You will be left with feeling a void in your heart, you will feel unfulfilled, and you will not be rewarded for it by Allah either, nor will you have the same motivation to keep going once it is achieved.

As Muslims, our main goals should be somehow or in some way related to our akhira (hereafter). Our goals should only be for the sake and pleasure of Allah. So, memorize the Quran because you want to please Allah and take your family and relatives to Jannah with you inshallah. Start a business or company to have more wealth to give to Islamic charities and for the advancement of Muslim communities or any good cause pleasing to Allah.

Be clear and precise about why exactly you have the goal that you do. Inshallah this will make it easier for you to stay motivated, because even in the midst of difficulties and turbulence, you will be able to navigate through it all and still stay on course towards your goals. This means that you must be intentional about what you do, and why you do it. All of your goals should be mission-based. There should be a purpose that transcends beyond yourself, and your reasons behind why it is you have a certain goal should truly be serving a greater purpose. Always renew your intentions and make sure they are only for the sake of Allah.

Eliminate Decision-making

Say "no" to any and all requests and invitations to extra projects that don't support your mission or objective. That means people you really love and care about have to be told, *"No."*

You want to prevent just wandering about idly. Even Allah said He didn't create us just to wander about the earth. So, why would we allow ourselves to run here and there, all the while neglecting and forsaking what is important to us and then to the community as a whole?

Having to make a lot of decisions daily is fatiguing to the brain. Practice saying no respectfully. At first, it is uncomfortable, and you don't want the recipient of your "no" to feel disappointed, but if you don't say no and make a habit of putting what is important to you first, then you will have so many projects and tasks that it will overwhelm you. It will take away from staying in the present, living meaningfully, and it will contribute to the hectic chaos many of us want to eliminate from our lives.

Practice saying no. Simplify your life to no more than one to two major goals daily. This will make it easier to stay focused and motivated inshallah.

Stay Committed

Any goal that you want to achieve requires commitment, even after the initial motivation has faded. You must build your self-discipline and get the work done whether you feel like it or not. So, focus on commitment, not motivation.

You must be committed to your goal, even if the sky falls apart or even if the earth breaks asunder. That is how committed you have to be to your goals, because if it is important to you, then there should be nothing that should ever hinder you or move you off track.

Staying committed to your goals is a responsibility. It makes you responsible for your behaviors. Therefore, it is really up to you to make sure that you take the necessary steps to achieve it. It is your behavior that ultimately results in a certain outcome. So technically, you are responsible for the behaviors and not the outcome, because the outcome is outside of your control and really up to Allah. Alhamdulillah, Allah always gives us even more than what we ask for or work for. So, don't worry about the outcome and stay committed to your goals by practicing certain behaviors that we discussed, which move you closer to your goals. Inshallah remain patient so Allah will take care of what is outside of your control for you.

Build a Community

Do you remember how anxious you felt in your school days if you didn't complete your homework? It was especially bad if you had a teacher who called you out on it in front of the whole classroom. So, you got all of your work done, because you didn't want to be seen as one of those lazy or useless students, and you wanted the teacher to think well of you. Okay, maybe you were a great student mashallah, but you must have known someone who slacked off in his or her work. Understanding the concept is what is important here, and it is one of accountability. Being supervised and asked about our work motivates us to get our tasks done, because it creates a bit of healthy pressure. You need to find someone who will hold you accountable and not accept any excuses you may have as to why you didn't accomplish your goal. They can be a tremendous help in getting ahead and becoming successful. We established previously that success and prosperity is linked to whom you associate with.

You need to have a community of people who will help support you in your pursuits. It can be your parents, teachers, or even your Twitter friends. The idea we must keep in mind here is to have a community of people that care about you and sincerely want to see you succeed. Having a group of people to support you and seek help from, especially in times of uncertainty and adversity, is incredibly helpful and accelerates the process of achieving your goals, because they will be there to help guide you inshallah.

Set High Standards for Yourself

Setting high standards and challenging ourselves gets the brain working to move us closer to the goals we have set for ourselves. You should expect greatness from yourself. After all, if Allah made you, there has to be many special and unique things about you that nobody else has.

You should not accept mediocrity of yourself when, for a fact, you know that you can be better. If you are doing less than you know you are capable of, then not only are you doing yourself a disservice, but you are also robbing your community and even the world of the gifts bestowed upon you by Allah.

Also, what you want to accomplish in the world doesn't have to be like other people's dreams and goals. If you want to be a good housewife, I would say, what could be more important? Just be the best at it, because even if you are at home, you are affecting the world. You will meet many people in your life who you can either have a positive impact on and bring them closer to Allah or you might influence them negatively and turn them away from Islam.

Human beings are always interacting and communicating, even in their absence and even in their silence. Your silence means something to someone. Your absence means something to someone, and they are intelligent enough to figure out why something is the way it is. So, whatever you choose to do with the number of days gifted to you by Allah and the high standards you have now set for yourself, make sure that they are spent in the service of Allah and His creation. It will come back to you many times inshallah.

Get Rid of Distractions

Turn off your phone, TVs, and any electronic devices that distract you. Try your best to stop browsing, and prevent the fatiguing of your brain. Eliminate or at least drastically reduce the number of decisions you make every single day. You can do that by not scrolling down your newsfeeds, or clicking on links and pages that don't contribute positively to your goals.

Ask yourself questions like, "How do I stay focused and on task?" Everyone has ways that are individual to him or her, so think about what helps you, then stick to it. Do not revert from it until you have finished your work.

Consistency is Key

Make a habit of getting your work done every day. We mentioned previously that the most beloved of deeds to Allah are the ones that are consistent, even if they are small. So, whether you want to memorize the Quran, do tahajjud (night prayer), or any other good deed, do it regularly. Consistency leads to momentum. Momentum makes you feel alive and makes you feel like you can do anything, as surely as you will inshallah.

Stop Telling Yourself That You Have Time

No one guarantees us the next moment, or the next day, let alone the next twenty years. Don't allow the delaying of your goals by saying you will do it someday. Why not do it today?

I know that it is an uncomfortable topic to talk about—us not living in this world forever—but it is the best motivator to getting our work done and achieving our goals. We can die at any moment, so we should make the best of the time given to us and work towards our goals now, instead of someday.

Time is the best commodity. Therefore, if you find yourself thinking you have so very little time, and you begin to spend it on worldly things, then stop yourself. If you are involved in anything that takes you away from Allah, then it is not worth doing at all. Choose your goals wisely, and spend the limited amount of time you have been given on them inshallah.

Don't Turn a Molehill into a Mountain

This happens, especially, when you let your work pile up. You become anxious and dread even going near what you have to do. You make every excuse to distance yourself from it, but the pile of tasks only grows more and becomes more daunting and scary.

I have noticed in myself and in others that when we let our tasks pile up, they seem to become harder to do. So, we don't end up doing them at all. It feels like you will fail so you don't end up trying at all. What is the solution to it all?

Just do it.

Get all of your work done as soon as possible. Get the most important and time-consuming tasks out of the way first. As you see that you're making progress, it will seem easier to you, because you have already done it and know what it takes.

Recognize Progress and Reward Yourself

When you make progress, it will make you want to achieve more. Your brain will be firing, and your dopamine and adrenaline will be ready to propel you forward towards accomplishing your tasks and getting you closer to your goals.

As you complete each task, recognize that you are closer and closer to your goal. Realizing that you have made progress will propel you further into focusing more and concentrating on your goal at hand. Progress makes you happy and ready to try again. For every task that you accomplish, even if it seems insignificant to you, label it as progress. It is incredibly important to feeling and staying motivated.

Then, as you reach certain milestones, reward yourself. Buy yourself ice cream, a nice kufi, or whatever makes you happy. Do it so you will come back to your goal more energized and pick up the pace. If you said that you would reward yourself after reaching a certain goal, do not allow yourself to feel guilty and then deprive yourself of the reward. You deserve to be treated kindly and rewarded, so go do whatever you told yourself you would do, and have fun doing it.

Break It Down

Some of our goals can seem like an insurmountable feat. So, if you find yourself feeling overwhelmed and stressed out, break down your goals to smaller, doable parts. Break it down to baby steps if that is what it takes. Divide it up in a way that is easy for you to do.

That being said, don't be so overly focused on your goal that it has a negative impact on your thoughts, and you become overwhelmed again. Go live life and do something fun so you are reenergized to try again.

Apply the 80/20 Rule

I first learned this rule from Brian Tracy, and it is just a phenomenal approach to getting things done, and you will notice that throughout this book, this rule has been alluded to many times. So, what is the 80/20 Rule? The 80/20 Rule is called the "Pareto Principle." It is named after its founder, Vilfredo Pareto, from 1895. This rule is incredibly helpful in staying motivated, and on task to achieving our goals and staying productive. This principle states that 20 percent of our activities determine 80 percent of our results. For example, if we have a list of ten things to do, then of those ten, only two things are of most importance to us. If we do those two things that are the most important or the hardest, then it will account for 80 percent of our results.

I found this principle to be a relief, because it shows that if we just focus on the two or three most important things in our day-to-day lives, we will increase our productivity, and get closer to our goals much more quickly instead of focusing on the many trivial and small tasks that we keep ourselves busy with. The application of this principle relieves us of stress and feeling overwhelmed, because we have so many things that we think we need to do, but don't have enough time to complete. This principle eliminates the idea of wanting to do everything, and feeling strained for time. Just do 20 percent, and reap 80 percent of the rewards. If we focus on applying this principle, we should find it easier to stay motivated and on track to achieving our goals inshallah.

Hopefully, you have found these tips helpful in staying motivated and focused so that you can make your *someday* a reality. Keep coming back to these tips, and reread them to motivate yourself once again. By nature, we are forgetful beings, so we will forget how to stay motivated and achieve certain tasks. Just revisit any points that you need to see again and continue on your journey to a beautiful life ahead of you inshallah.

Salahtul-Istikhara

Before you begin the journey to achieving a positive mindset, take Allah as a friend. Whenever you're trying to do anything by yourself, you won't be able to. But when Allah is with you, anything is possible. Therefore, do not delay in asking Allah and seek His guidance. Do salatul-istikhara. This is a voluntary prayer to seek Allah's guidance between permissible alternatives. This means that we should not be asking Allah's help in un-Islamic things, but only use it in situations that are permissible for us.

Do two rak'ahs (units) of extra (nafl) salah, seeking guidance, ease and help from Allah. It is extremely important and I have seen its benefits in my own life. It is from the sunnah of the Prophet, peace be upon him.

We learn from Riyad Al-Saliheen that Jabir ibn Abdullah, may Allah be pleased with him, said: "The Prophet, peace be upon him, used to teach us to seek Allah's Counsel in all matters, as he used to teach us a surah from the Qur'an. He would say: When anyone of you has an important matter to decide, let him pray two rak'ahs other than the obligatory prayer, and then say:
'Oh Allah, verily, I seek your guidance with your knowledge. And I seek Your Strength from Your Might, I ask from Your Great Blessings, because

You have Power and I do not, You Know everything and I do not know, and You have knowledge of the unseen. Oh Allah! If in Your Knowledge, this (name what you are seeking guidance for) ------------------ is better for my religion, and my life and end [death], then make it destined for me and make it easy for me and then put blessings [barakah] in it for me. O Allah! In Your Knowledge, if this affair (name what you are seeking guidance for) ------------------- is bad for me, in my religion, and my life and end [death], then turn it away from me and turn me away from it and whatever is better for me, ordain [destine] it for me, then make me pleased with it.'"

After you have done your two rak'ah nafl prayer, praise Allah, send peace, blessings and salutations upon the Prophet, peace be upon him, and make the dua of istikhara. This is so that we follow the correct etiquette of making dua to Allah. How would you approach a king in this world, especially if you were about to make a request from him? Most likely you would humble yourself, lower your head, dress in the cleanest of clothes and in the best way possible. You would speak in a way that he could comprehend what you were saying, and witness your humility. You would praise him first and mention his excellent characteristics and qualities.

Allah is more deserving of being approached in this way than any king of this world, because Allah is the King of all kings. To Allah belong all kingdoms. So praise Allah first, and praise and ask for blessings for the one He loves the most, which is the Prophet, peace be upon him, then make the dua of istikhara.

You can make the dua in your own language as well if you don't know it in Arabic, although you can find it easily online. Salatul Istikhara is especially helpful if you are unsure of what path to take and which goals to pursue. Do istikhara, then whatever decision you feel is most right to take, then do so, and you will not regret it. Have full and complete trust that Allah will guide you and provide help to you.

Be absolutely sure that Allah's guidance and mercy will reach you, and find a way out for you. Think only good things of Allah, and expect the best from Him, and it will surely be bestowed upon you.

To recap, in this book we discussed what the Muslim mindset is and its importance. We discussed that the first step to having a Muslim mindset is to have a strong eman as discussed in Lesson 1. This can be accomplished by correcting our belief in Allah and taking courses from upright scholars to make sure what we believe about Allah is true.

In Lesson 1, we also learned how to strengthen our eman by fulfilling the fard and all the necessary acts of worship such as prayers, fasting, and wearing a hijab. We need to make dua, recite Quran, and spend time in solitude with Allah in dhikr. We need to think about the blessings bestowed upon us.

Lesson 2 was forming good relationships with our parents. Practicing humility is an important aspect to achieving good relationships with our parents, allowing us to benefit from their wisdom and knowledge, and enhancing our ability to achieve the Muslim mindset.

Lesson 3 was in regards to having meaningful relationships with our friends, community members, and mentors. We need to be wary of the types of people we choose to associate with, because they are our future and their future is what ours will look like as well.

Lesson 4 was the establishment of the necessity of forgiveness of ourselves, and other people. It included simple daily exercises we can implement so that we can finally let go.

Lesson 5 was about keeping your health and wellbeing intact. You really cannot be good to anyone if you are not good to yourself. Your health affects your mindset greatly, and if it is in good condition, it will propel you towards your goals and pursuits. Bad health will hinder you from worshipping Allah, and contribute to a negative mindset.

Lesson 6 was about thinking positive. This is where you actively control your thoughts and become very observant about what you think. Try to get to the bottom of the reasoning behind your thoughts. Thinking positive is a very powerful practice, and it leads to exponentially good results in terms of progression towards goals and having an optimistic viewpoint.

Lesson 7 was a look into waking up early. This lesson is filled with practical everyday tips and tricks you can use right away to help you wake up and strive towards achieving a positive mindset inshallah. Waking up early is the practice of many influential and successful people.

Lesson 8 was all about one of the greatest forms of meditation and a practice that will instantly make you feel better, which is gratitude. It is the shaper of your beliefs and of your world. Gratitude is a necessary part of a Muslim's life.

LESSON 10: EXECUTE YOUR GOALS

Lesson 9 was about patience. Patience during adversity, in obedience to Allah, and in avoiding sins is an important practice and can help one achieve success by harnessing the ability to endure even when one feels like giving up.

Lesson 10 is to state your goal, make a plan as to how you will execute your goals, and then get the work done. Execution can be argued as one of the most powerful steps in achieving a positive mindset, because the results are tangible and often measurable.

You are on an incredible journey to discovering yourself, achieving your goals, and maintaining a positive mindset. You will have many ups and many downs. Some days you will feel great, while other days you will wonder if it is even worth it. I promise you it is worth every step. I usually don't make any promises to anyone, but this I am sure of. You have the abilities and the power within you to become who you were always meant to be. Be patient through the difficulties, obstacles, and challenges, and you will overcome. You will prevail.

Just as the sun rises every morning, so shall you rise too. You have within you the gifts of striving, overcoming, and being what you were born to be. You will figure it out. Keep at it every day. Keep learning, practicing, and striving. Never stop. Never give up.

You can be extraordinary. You can achieve so much greatness that you barely recognize yourself. Change your life and then help others along the way.

You now have enough knowledge to excel in your chosen endeavors. Please promise that you won't lose hope in yourself or your abilities. Most importantly, please don't lose hope in the only one capable of change, help, guidance, and transformation, and He is Allah. Always turn to Him, even if you feel like you have a good handle on things. Allah is never far. He is closer to you than your jugular vein.

I am confident that you will succeed, and one day you will become who you were always meant to be even if you feel like that is not possible. I am confident that you can transform not only yourself, but your surroundings as well and the lives of many who will enter your life inshallah.

Be at ease and be not worried about the outcomes. Focus on what you can do to make your goals and dreams a reality, and then take action. Allah will take care of the rest for you inshallah.

I will end with what I started with and it is that the Prophet, peace be upon him said, "Allah, the Exalted said, 'I am as My servant thinks I am (expects me to be). I am with him when he mentions Me. If he mentions Me to himself, I mention him to Myself; and if he mentions me in an assembly, I mention him in an assembly greater than it (the gathering of the angels). If he draws near to me a hand's length, I draw near to him an arm's length. And if he comes to me walking, I go to him running."

Therefore, be not ever saddened nor deterred when any difficult situation arises or when doubts creep in, because Allah will come to you running. Keep steadfast to the way of Allah, His Messenger and Prophet Mohammad, peace be upon him, and the way of the righteous people that followed after him. They practiced and maintained the best mindset. The Muslim mindset.

****

May Allah grant us the ability to apply what we have learned, and transform our lives for the better inshallah. May Allah be pleased with every one of us and grant us the pleasure of seeing His face.
Ameen.

WILL YOU DO ME A FAVOR, PLEASE?

If you have enjoyed *The Muslim Mindset*, would you mind taking a minute to write a review on Amazon? Even a short review helps and it would mean a lot to me.

If someone you care about has been struggling with a negative mindset, or wants to learn to achieve a positive Muslim mindset, please send him or her a copy of this book.

Finally, if you'd like to receive updates on my future projects, books and blog posts, you can sign up for my newsletter at ZakiaKhalil.com.

You can also find me on Twitter @IamZakiaKhalil and Facebook @iamzakiakhalil.

Thank you.

Glossary

Akhira: The hereafter, life after death

Alhamdulillah: Praise be to Allah

Allah: God, the only deity worthy of worship

Ameen : [Oh Allah] Let it be.

Barakah: Blessings

Dawah: To call people to Islam

Dhikr: Remembrance of God

Dua: Supplication, beseeching God

Fard: Obligatory acts of worship

Fajr: Dawn Prayer

Hadith: Sayings, actions, habits, and various collections from the life of Prophet Mohammad, peace be upon him

Haram: Unlawful according to Islam

Inshallah: If Allah wills

Jannah: The Garden or Paradise in which the Believers
will live in the hereafter.

Juz: One part of the Quran

Khutba: A sermon given on the holy day of Friday

Kufi: A cap Muslim men wear

Mashallah: Just as Allah wished

Nafl: Voluntary extra prayers

Prophet Mohammad: The final messenger sent to all of mankind, received revelation of the Quran

Quran: The recitation, a revelation sent to Prophet Mohammad, peace be upon him

Rabb: Lord

Rak'ah: A unit of prayer

Salah: Prayer (refers to the five daily prayers Muslims pray)

Shaitan: Satan

Sunnah: The beliefs, sayings, actions, approvals and way of the Prophet Mohammad, peace be upon him

Surah: A chapter of the Quran. There are 114 chapters in the Quran.

Tahajjud: Voluntary night prayer that is loved by Allah

Wajib: Obligatory or mandatory acts of worship

Wudhu: A ritual purification of washing of the face, limbs, and wiping over the head

Zakat: Obligatory charity in Islam

Bibliography

Al-Bulandshehri, Shaykh Ashiq Ilahi. *Provisions for the Seekers,* translated by Ibn Yusuf, Abdur-Rahman. Santa Barbara. White Thread Press. 2009. Print. 41-42.

Al-Hafiz, Ibn Kathir. *The Exegesis of the Grand Holy Quran.* Beirut. Dar Al-Kotob Al-Ilmiyah. 2006. Print.

Al-Nawawi, Imam Muhyu Al-Din Abu Zakariya Ibn Yahya Ibn Sharaf. *Riyad Al-Saliheen.* Lahor. Maktaba-e-Rehmania. Print.

Dr. Al-Bugha, Mostafa. *Al-Wafa.* Beirut. Dar ibn Kathir. 2003. Print. 15.

Dr. Dweck, Carol S. *Mindset: The New Psychology of Success.* New York. Penguin-Random House. 2006. Print.

Enright, Robert. *Effects of Forgiveness Therapy on Anger, Mood and Vulnerability to Substance Abuse Among Inpatient Substance-Dependent Clients.* The American Psychological Association. 2004. Print. 72, No. 6, 1114-1121.

Flynn, Pat. "Niche Site Duel: Finding a Profitable Niche: My Process Revealed." *TheSmartPassiveIncome.com.* Flynndustries, LLC. 18 August 2010. Web. 4 June 2017.

Ibn Humaid, Saleh ibn Abdullah and Ibn Malluh, Abdur-Rahman ibn Mohammad ibn Abdur-Rahman. *Nadrat An-Naim.* Jeddah. Dar Al-Wasilah. 2004. Print. Vol. 3. 2441.

"Parkinson's Law," *BrianTracy.com.* Brian Tracy International. Web. 7 July 2017.

"The 80 20 Rule Explained." *BrianTracy.com.* Brian Tracy International. Web. 4 June 2017.

Made in the USA
Middletown, DE
26 June 2020